Lord, Take Care of Me!

Lord, Take Care of Me!

STORIES OF GOD'S HEALING
OF ABUSED CHILDREN AT

Camp Alandale

A Christian camp for abused children

KAREN WOOD

WINEPRESS WP PUBLISHING

Printed in the United States of America.

Cover Design by Karen Wood and Ragont Design.

Edited by Susan Titus Osborn

Preliminary editing by Tina Massa, Marni Loth, and Heather Fuqua.

Final proof reading by Mary Harris, Nancy Hurtt, Stella Johnson, Anne Moore, Alice Rafidi, Joan Wood, and Marilyn Horton.

ISBN 1-57921-462-2
Library of Congress Catalog Card Number: 2002102700

Explanation of Book Cover

The book cover is a watercolor painting done by the author. The scene shows a forest with pine trees like those that surround Camp Alandale. A night, with a full moon, is detailed with sheep on the bottom front cover to give the idea of the care they must be having even though it is dark. If there are sheep, surely the shepherd is nearby, surely there is danger lurking also. The title of the book is *Lord, Take Care of Me!* The picture illustrates that even if the sheep, the abused child, look like they are alone and abandoned by others in the largeness of darkness, the Lord in reality, is still nearby caring for them.

Title of the Book

The title of the book, *Lord, Take Care of Me!* is based on Psalm 27:10, a favorite verse used at Camp Alandale:

> *When my father and mother forsake me, then the Lord will take care of me.* (NKJV)

Name Changes

Most of the names of the children in this book have been changed to protect their privacy.

Acknowledgments

I would like to thank Tina Massa, Marni Loth, and Heather Fuqua for the preliminary editing of this book. And I would like to thank Susan Titus Osborn for the content editing. I would also like to thank Senator Rob and Nancy Hurtt for their part in making this book possible.

Table of Contents

Introduction 9
1. How Did Camp Alandale Begin? 11
2. A Camper Named Steve 15
3. Geronimo 21
4. Maria's Prayers 24
5. Charity's Story 30
6. Flames of Healing 32
7. Reynaldo's Testimony 36
8. Our "Kids" Grow Up! 45
9. Ti's Anchor 47
10. We Get Letters 50
11. Brother and Sister Reconciled 54
12. God's Faithfulness to Jenny 58
13. From Foe to Friend 61
14. The Power of Prayer 63
15. Joanne, God's Ambassador 66
16. In God's Time 72
17. Terrorism: Satan's Tool 75
18. God's Second Purpose 78
19. From Fear to Trust 82
20. Keri Tells Her Story 87
21. Dana Shares Her Testimony 92
22. What Happens at Camp? 96
23. Answers to Prayer 102
24. Adult Campers Return 108

Afterword 111

Appendix A Glossary 112
Appendix B How to Contact Us or Get Involved 114
Appendix C Statistics of Abuse and How Camp Helps 117
Appendix D How to Help a Hurting Person Without Getting Hurt 120
Appendix E How to Report Abuse 126

This book is dedicated to
the children
who have attended Camp Alandale

Though my father and mother forsake me, the LORD will receive me.
(Psalm 27:10)

Know therefore that the LORD your God is God; he is the faithful God, keeping his covenant of love to a thousand generations of those who love him and keep his commands. (Deuteronomy 7:9)

I will sing of the LORD'S great love forever; with my mouth I will make your faithfulness known through all generations. (Psalm 89:1)

Introduction

My body felt chilled by the night air as I sat there listening. My insides felt even colder as I heard her story. She sat staring at the campfire as if eye contact would be too much to bear. Horror after horror had happened to her. First her dad, then her stepdad, then her grandfather had molested her. In time, one by one, they each abandoned her. Even her mother ended up choosing drugs over her own daughter.

My heart could not handle all the feelings and was gripped even more as she continued. She was put in the county system where the siblings she had raised since she was five were ripped out of her life. They were each scattered to different foster and group homes. At this point of her story her sobs became the most piercing. Her sister was so distraught over the separation that she ran away from her group home never to be seen again. Her brothers she only saw once or twice a year. Her youngest brother, "her baby" that she raised from infancy, was adopted. At the request of the adoptive family, she was never allowed to see him again. She was moved through twenty foster homes in four years because of her displays of anger. She could not understand why "everything" had happened to her.

In spite of all this, she decided to forgive everyone who had hurt her as well as to give her pain to Jesus and put it all behind her.

In order to understand this breakthrough let's back track and look at the event that turned this girl's head. At campfire her counselor, Susan, shared her testimony. She had treated Susan badly, but then found that her counselor's life paralleled her own life. During the "one-on-one" time (refer to Appendix A, "Glossary," page 113) following her counselor's testimony, she poured out her heart and shared all that had happened to her. They cried and held each other, feeling God's presence grow.

At that point she knew God was real and asked Jesus to take control of her life. The next night she courageously shared her testimony at campfire. Everyone's response of hugs and comfort began her healing.

There are so many stories of healing like this to share that we felt we needed to write this book. The stories are horrific: threats with knives and guns, young boys hitting their own fathers over the head with baseball bats or 2 x 4s to protect a sister or mother. Some have been literally thrown through walls or out windows; others have heard threats of suicide from their parents. Still others have witnessed parents overdosing or putting a gun to their own head and pulling the trigger.

When our spirits are overwhelmed with sorrow, we see the amazing power of Jesus touching the bruised and bringing healing. Nearly all of the children that share their abuse with us have ended up giving their hearts to Jesus. Hundreds have left camp with a large measure of healing of their profoundly deep wounds. How can that happen? We never stop asking that same question even though we see it so often.

We continue to see incredible growth in returning campers, too. Many have a consistent, growing walk with God. We know it is due to the intense prayer coverage by our teams of churches (26 churches as of this writing). Through the years, we have gained such confidence and constant warmth in the knowledge of this prayer coverage. It is the most needed gift for these children who are battling against the odds and against Satan to be free.

We are in constant warfare for the healing of hearts and souls. When things get tough, as they often do, we are sure it is only the prayers of so many that keep us all from buckling under. Without prayer, the campers would go unreached and could go on to be abusers, criminals, and psychopaths in our society causing untold harm.

While witnessing the strength of God to reach the unreachable, we have felt a responsibility to share with others what God has done. These stories may help someone who needs to hear that there is healing possible even for them through God's love. Others need to hear how God works for the good of His own children especially through their horrific pain. Many need to know that He has not forgotten them, nor is He unfair or unjust. May all who read this book allow God to bless, encourage, and strengthen them.

Sincerely Yours,
Karen Wood for the Camp Alandale Family

Chapter One

How Did Camp Alandale Begin?

One of the most frequently asked questions is, "How did Camp Alandale begin?" My husband, Robin, and my walk of faith all began when I was involved with a cult that had caused us to have numerous fights about religion. Our marriage began to dissolve. Because of these arguments and the tension, Robin decided to get away for a weekend by himself to try and figure out what to do. While in a campground, a perfect stranger shared Jesus with him. Robin found the answer he was looking for, though it was not what he expected.

Sadly, the marriage struggles continued. In an attempt to find common ground, Robin suggested that we go to a non-denominational church for a year to study the Bible apart from organized religion. To us that meant neutral ground. We started attending Coast Bible Church. We were greeted by Hyatt and Anne Moore who invited themselves into our home to do weekly Bible studies. At that time, they had been missionaries with Wycliffe Bible Translators for five years.

One Sunday, Coast Bible church had a past cult member share why he had left the cult. I was instantly frightened since I had been told, "Watch out for emissaries of Satan who will come along to confuse you." I was immediately praying and told God, "I will not go to this man, Lord. You must bring him to me so I know whether he is from you."

As the service closed, all that the guest speaker, Mr. Guindon, had said was ringing in my ears. He left the podium and sat right behind me with his family. A natural conversation began that lasted the rest of the day. Three days later I finished reading all the materials he had given to me.

The weeks had flown by studying the Bible with the Moores. The Moores had missionaries from all over the world and members of Coast Bible Church praying for us. The Spirit was already working in Robin and me in a powerful way. We had been studying the book of Romans but all the lights were turned on for me from what Mr. Guindon had given me to read. I accepted the Lord with Robin and Anne that third day (Hyatt was out of town with

Wycliffe business). Soon we were in three Bible studies and each of us was teaching one ourselves to neighbors and co-workers.

The example of Hyatt and Anne's walk of faith drew our hearts to want their kind of life. The excitement of all the answers to prayers in regard to their missionary work and for their family further captured us and inspired us. In three short years we were praying that we would also be able to give our whole selves in a work for the Lord. We sought the Lord's will. Opportunities seemed to materialize and vanish. When we were completely yielded to whatever God had for us, things began to happen, yet not at all as we had envisioned.

In 1980 the call of God finally focused on starting a camp for *underprivileged* children. At first it seemed crazy. We had never worked with children, although I loved and had always hoped to work with them. We had no camp experience except for Robin going to a school camp in the sixth grade. Furthermore, Robin had, in the past, expressed that he did not even like children, except his own!

But as the months went by, it became evident that God was leading us to do this by faith. Our church was not quite ready to support our work. It did not seem wise to them for us to start a ministry since we had only been Christians for four years. Hyatt and Anne, however, who had tried to interest us in Wycliffe were supportive. They could see we were doing this as an act of faith and trusting God to lead.

God had done a work in our hearts. We were willing to give up all our "toys" and our Orange County life. The Moores' example spoke deeply within, creating conviction. The Moores lived simply and by what God provided. Our Porsche had been an idol to us, but we sold it. The ski boat that was the symbol of seeking our own personal satisfaction was given to my sister. Our large Orange County house was eventually sold to buy a home in the mountains to hold camp. Soon, Karen's business of making uniforms for fancy restaurants and Robin's Newport office with an ocean view did not hold the glamour they once did. They were meaningless in comparison to being able to follow Jesus and reach others!

God confirmed our choices in ways too numerous to recount. One choice, however, spoke to all who wondered if we had gone off the deep end. We had decided that Robin would give one-month's notice at his work, and then we would trust God to provide our income. We had no other plan or job lined up.

We knew God had called and we were willing to go and wait on His providence. We also wanted to be self-supporting and did not intend to raise our support as others usually did. You can imagine how naive and foolish we seemed to family and friends! But we wanted all the donations given to go toward reaching the children.

Robin had been a valuable employee as a systems analyst for the Irvine Company. When Robin turned in his resignation, his boss asked him how he planned to earn a living. When he heard our plans to start a camp, he asked if Robin would consider being a consultant for the Irvine Company.

It so happened that his boss was in charge of hiring all the consultants. He offered him a consultant job two days a week, working ten hours a day, and suggested that he return the next day with a salary amount in mind. When Robin returned and told him the amount that we calculated we would need to survive, his boss responded, saying, "That would never do."

When Robin said, "Well, we cannot survive on less and . . ." His boss cut him off and said, "It is not that it is too much. It is too little. If you are going to be a consultant with the Irvine Company, you have to charge a lot more or they will think you are not good enough. Let's double the amount!" Robin ended up earning more income than he had made on salary working overtime!

Robin's job worked well as we started a ministry. He consulted a couple days a week and we used the rest of the time on family and camp. This new way of life and a new walk of faith were exciting but we were faced with working with each other full time. After the honeymoon, one of the first times we tried to work together was in the garden. It was a disaster. Robin insisted I was holding the hoe incorrectly. It was decided we would not do projects together! We are as opposite in our approaches as God makes personalities.

I was eager and excited about starting a camp. I was motivated and empowered. Robin, however, felt the huge responsibility of it all and worried about his fear of children. I am always ready to do things yesterday, while Robin thinks things through with great prudence and wisdom.

To Robin, tomorrow is always a better day to make a clear decision. It is true that opposites attract! But the blend (even if it got steamy) was perfect for the ministry. I inspired Robin, and Robin kept me from getting too extreme. We had a built-in monitor which kept us from jumping too fast or waiting too long. Robin admits that if it had not been for me saying, "I did not come up here to plan and wait for buildings for two years before we have children here," we would have probably never thought of tents and running camps that first year in 1980. Robin, I admit with admiration, keeps the ministry stable and sane.

As we considered having camp, we knew people camp all the time in tents and barbecue their food over open fires. Why couldn't the campers be taught how to make their own food as they learned some camping skills? So Robin found out about an army surplus auction where he found large tents. I planned a camping menu and program. We invited underprivileged children from the inner cities of Santa Ana and Los Angeles, and even the Banning Indian reservation. Friends started giving us leads on transportation, food, and insurance. One couple we never heard from again showed up and gave us a bullhorn the first day of camp. That was a necessity we did not even know we needed. We saw providence in every stage that had brought us to the time for camp to begin!

Chapter Two

A Camper Named Steve

At our first camp, we felt like we were standing on a skinny tree limb that might break at any moment, and yet we felt God's overwhelming leading and support. God had obviously brought everything together. He granted one miracle after another.

When the bus arrived with our first group of campers, both the energized and overwhelmed feelings were high. We soon noticed a young man, Steve, who had been pushed on the bus at the pick-up, then was pushed off the bus and the door closed when he got to camp! We soon saw he was in a catatonic state, unable to relate to his world. I had heard of such conditions where a person decides to lose consciousness and feeling, so as not to relate to his world. We later learned that he had closed out everything because of several traumas he had endured. We did not have experience or education in how to handle a situation like this. We had just planned to have a camp for children who came from *disadvantaged* backgrounds. We had not planned on dealing with a child like this who we later found out had been sexually abused by a man.

He was assigned to a counselor named Dave Blackford who had to lead him or push him to every event. He even had to hand feed him. By that evening Dave was baffled by Steve and frustrated with himself. His rattled self-confidence and exhausted spirit drove him to have a talk with me, "Karen, what am I doing wrong? How do I reach him? Am I ruining him?" These questions all tumbled out.

My mind raced with prayers to God. "I need to know what to tell him, Lord. We are supposed to be the directors, and Dave expects me to have an answer!" The thought went through my head, "Tell Dave just to love him, and that he is doing fine." I pushed the thought aside and frantically pleaded for God to give an answer, since the first thought seemed to be too simple. I thought I needed something profound to say!

When the exact thought went through my head again Dave was through talking and waiting for me to say something. With all the confidence I could muster, I told Dave, "I can see that you are doing all you can. You have not done anything wrong. Don't give up." Then with all the passion I could muster, I said, "Just keep loving him, Dave!" Dave looked at me as if a light had been turned on, said okay, and walked away with a determined walk.

God had picked the most patient and loving counselor we had to give to Steve. God used this special man to reach into the heart of this broken child. At our last evening campfire, we asked the campers to share what they had learned during the three days they were with us.

We were all shocked when Steve stood up and started talking! He had not spoken a single word during the entire camp. He said, "Now I know what love is. Love is giving not taking. The man who used me said he loved me, but that is not love. When I grow up I'm going to be a counselor at Camp Alandale."

We couldn't believe what God had done, but it did not end there. The people in Orange County Social Services were all overwhelmed by Steve's recovery. They explained his condition and history to us. What two years in therapy had not done was accomplished by God in a three-day camp. They wanted to know who we were. Eventually they asked if we would be willing to take all the children from Orange County Social Services for a camp experience! Because of Steve, the door was open for a Christian ministry to receive children from a governmental organization.

We will never forget Steve. Steve showed us that God is able to teach and use ordinary people. Our motto rose from this: "God doesn't always call the qualified. God qualifies the called." So, we have always looked for God's called servants more than trained counselors for this work. Because of God's faithfulness and His work in Steve, the doors to Orange County were opened, and they have been open ever since. God also taught us through Steve that *HIS love* is the answer for the most hurting children. Our main job is to love children with Christ's love and to love unconditionally and to persevere in that job.

Steve also brought the focus of what our ministry was to be—ministering to abused children. Our vision is to reach children all over Southern California and across the nation someday. The purpose of Camp Alandale is to expose abused and neglected children to the life-changing and healing reality of Jesus Christ and to help equip them to have meaningful, productive lives.

For two years Steve continued to attend Camp Alandale, and he was a real blessing as he grew in the Lord. But one summer he did not return to camp, and when we called and questioned his brother we found out that everyone believed he had been abducted by his original abuser. For a year he was missing and no one knew where he was. Later we learned from

Steve that he had been used as a slave. He was kept in rooms with no windows so he could not escape. He had no fresh air, and no sunlight for a year. Finally, he escaped. However, when he saw daylight again he looked up to heaven and said, "If this is what being Christian is all about, I do not want anything to do with you, God." He was blaming God for not protecting him. He decided to turn toward drugs, girls, and stealing. Within a year his life was in even more of a mess. He was homeless, almost dead from disease, and running from people who wanted to kill him because of a $10,000 debt he owed.

In his lowest moment he said, "God, I tried it my way but that has not worked either. If You are real, will You come and find me?" Instantly, Steve said he felt like he could feel a huge bubble of blessings that God was ready to pour on him just above his head. As he asked for God's help it seemed like the bubble burst, and the warm arms of God wrapped around him. He instantly knew God had been there with the blessings ready to give him all along, but God was just waiting for him to ask. He had indescribable peace and the knowledge that he was going to be all right.

Within a few short months Steve's health returned, he obtained a good job, and he was out of debt, plus, the "hit" on his life was removed. He could not believe the miracle from God he had witnessed himself. He resolutely made up his mind that he would never doubt God's ways in the future, and he would never walk away from his Savior again.

Steve had always said he was going to honor his promise as a child and be a counselor at Camp Alandale, but a couple years after getting married he moved to Washington State and then on to Oklahoma. He calls from time to time and reconfirms that desire and how he is just waiting on God's timing.

Steve endured another tragedy—the death of a son, two years after his marriage at age twenty. Convinced by his knowledge that God does things better than he, Steve accepted this tragedy as God's plan and was not shaken but strengthened by it! He and his wife Karen were an amazing example to many at their church and to co-workers. This was because of Steve's decision to never doubt God's ways again. Before he married Karen, he asked her to make the same commitment to God or he could not marry her. In this tragedy, they were both unwavering!

Remembering Steve's testimony reminds us where we have been in Christ's strength, and where we are going. Yet there is so much left to do. Jesus reassures us that it is more than worth the sacrifices. He teaches us of what He is deeply accomplishing in each camper's life.

The following is Steve's letter for others who are going through trials.

Dear Campers,

It seems all of my life before becoming a Christian I felt numb. It started with my first loss of my pet cat. I learned to have no feelings. Not until now—I am 30–can I see I have not needed to be afraid of emotions. In the past my emotions were so full of anger that I was afraid I would hurt someone if they came out. If I didn't show emotion I would not lose control or become violent. I felt nothing. It was scary thinking about it. I would always ask myself what is wrong with you? Now I am not the same person. I am free!!!

I remember when I froze up. I was standing trying not to think, just after court let out where the molestation had come out. It froze me. That was the way I was at camp. I remember being frozen and numb.

I remember being at the table by our tent when Dave Blackford took me to the side by the bushes. He asked me very simply about asking Jesus into my life, and I wanted to. I couldn't tell Dave, but I just did it! It was that simple but very real. Everything changed from that moment on. I remember getting lost on the hike along the river. I prayed to God to help me find a way back. And I knew that when I got back that He had done it. I remember I scared everyone because I was lost, but I felt very secure in Jesus.

God has done some amazing things in my life through Camp Alandale and since then. My wife, Karen knew the Lord, too, and had some hard times in her life. But when she was four months pregnant she had our baby prematurely. He had a rare genetic disease that caused his liver not to function properly. He died only after living for four months. We loved him so much. It was really hard losing him but we clung to each other and to the Lord. God was faithful.

Because of wanting to live in a less crowded and less expensive state, we moved to Washington. It was a good move, except that I was out of work for a year and a half, there. Karen worked, and I was a full time dad. It was great. I cannot look at a job the same way anymore. My main work will always be at home. Your family needs you, first. Eventually, we knew it was God's will as we were squeezed to only one option-moving to Oklahoma.

We found a great church full of loving and caring people and have really grown in the Lord since we started going. I found a good job and there are several Christians at work so I fellowship there, too.

I decided a long time ago that I am going on with my life. I am not going to live in the past. Life is great now! And I would not be who I am without the bad experiences God allowed. I have meaning and a reason to rejoice everyday. So much so that people are always asking me, "Why are you so happy?" Especially the people at work ask as I come in all happy early in the morning. I can say I experienced a living hell before, so now each day literally holds so much to be thankful for.

Often people come to me to share their problems. I will share with people any hurt I have suffered no matter how embarrassing, if they need it and will listen. After my story they always really end up opening up. I can actually help them see God in things.

So, the way Karen and I look at it is that we are survivors whose lives have gone the way they have so we can help others. I feel God has much more to do with my life. I am just at the beginning of using my past!

When I was young I thought that I just wanted to be rich. But now my work has only one purpose-to provide for my family and to witness to people. My real goals revolve around doing things for others. That is my focus. Nothing else can take the place of God. When you come to the level where God's love is real to you it becomes the most important thing on earth. The ultimate is that we can use it to help others. We offer simple choices to them, and people do not have to go to hell! If we do not have faith and take a leap, people stay lost. I have found that people amazingly want answers so I need to step out and help. I keep seeing people who want what the Lord has to offer, and all we need to do is to just share!

I have lost everything I had three times. I can earn a lot of money if I want. Now I thank God for the loses because it helped me see clearly how you never lose God no matter what you go through. I still cannot see the forest for the trees sometimes, but I just refocus God. I used to keep crashing because of "dirty goggles." The problem was never on God. It was me and my "dirty goggles" or view of life. When I finally realized that I needed to take off the goggles, I saw God and the door that was there open all the time to reach Him.

Karen is perfectly made for me. We have the same mind set. We now have two children. Rachel is five and Michael is one. Going through these together has made us and our marriage stronger.

I want to tell the campers not to forget to LIVE the things we learned at camp. Tell them that I know that God is there through everything and will never leave them.

Love,
Steve

Steve's life is a dramatic demonstration of how God works good out of the evil of this world. God could prevent all abuse, but then He would eliminate man's free will. God wanted the people of His creation to be able to choose Him, instead of being forced to do so. It was not His will that His creation with free will would fall into sin and ruin the perfect world He gave to Adam and Eve. From Scripture we realize God foresaw all the evil that man would choose to do and included it in His plan.

And we know that in all things God works for the good of those who love him, who have been called according to his purpose. (Romans 8:28)

God could have ignored us and left us to our just reward. But God chose to graciously provide redemption freely to us, by the extreme suffering and death of His own Son.

For God so loved the world that he gave his one and only Son, that whoever believes in him shall not perish but have eternal life. For God did not send his Son into the world to condemn the world, but to save the world through him. (John 3:16–17)

We also learn from Steve that what we suffer, even as innocent children, can be used by God to give us full wonderful lives.

For our light and momentary troubles are achieving for us an eternal glory that far outweighs them all. (2 Corinthians 4:17)

When God foresaw what Steve would be subjected to in this world, He chose him to be the one who would set the course of the ministry of Camp Alandale and the person who would be in the right place eventually to reach many.

God has many rewards for those who can accept the way in which He will use their lives. That reward far outweighs the pain. And that reward is one, as sinners, we do not even deserve. But God is kind and loving and merciful.

He will wipe every tear from their eyes. There will be no more death or mourning or crying or pain, for the old order of things has passed away. (Revelation 21:4)

Chapter Three

Geronimo

When we first started camp, we invited children from the local Indian Reservation. We developed a close relationship with a Bible teaching pastor who had a church on the reservation. He was excited to send the children he knew but had to convince their parents that a camp experience would be beneficial to them. In at least a dozen families he was able to eliminate their distrust of the white man.

One child who came was named Geronimo. Yes, his real name was Geronimo. When Geronimo arrived at camp he was an angry child who was used to bullying his way through situations. Later we found out he was called "Champ" at his school because he had never lost a fight. He bullied all the students at school which caused them to be afraid of him. Even we were intimidated by his tough exterior. Yet we continued to share the love of the Lord with him.

At the end of a teaching session, we asked the children who wanted to accept the Lord to raise their hands. We had all the children close their eyes. We were in awe when we saw that Geronimo's hand was raised up high. We told all the children who had raised their hands to go to the other room where someone would talk with them about their decisions.

Geronimo was so torn by his decision, he struggled to stand up, put his feet under him, and go to the other room. Finally, as those of us with our eyes opened prayed we knew God's Spirit prodded him. Geronimo got up and shuffled into the other room. There he made a sincere profession of faith and commitment to the Lord.

Geronimo continued to come to camp the next two years. Then he moved away. We learned from him that he had come from an abusive home with parents who stayed drunk most of the time. All the Indians on his reservation (adults and children) received a quarterly check of around $5000 from the bingo/gaming business that was run on their reservation. As he shared, we learned that all the adults in his life seldom worked and would waste their money.

His disclosure amazed us as he described children who could buy motorcycles or other big toys with every check. Their parents usually bought drugs and alcohol. The homes were run down shacks and mobile homes dressed up with expensive stereos and televisions on the inside. At this very young age, he was bored with these things, and his future looked hopeless. He was sure he could never better himself or leave the reservation.

He said that his lack of motivation as he depended on an unearned income "trapped him and all the others." Geronimo's understanding of having any kind of a future and planning for it was non-existent. Yet, the principles presented at camp opened a whole new world to him and gave him hope.

Geronimo went home and immediately led his younger brother to the Lord. Eventually, he led his sisters and father to the Lord. The pastor from the church said that after attending camp Geronimo came to church for the first time and continued faithfully thereafter. Slowly but surely he brought everyone in his family to church except his mother. Sadly, she eventually left the family because she couldn't stand all of them turning to Jesus. We heard that his family moved after this so we lost track of him.

The pastor said that when Geronimo came to church he would sing the worship songs with all his heart while he cried out loud with tears flowing down his cheeks. Geronimo told the pastor, "I can feel the tears clean me of all the bad stuff I did." At school he never fought again and thus developed a whole new reputation. With the kind of change and healing God performed in Geronimo, we are confident that *he who began a good work in (him) will carry it on to completion until the day of Christ Jesus* (Philippians 1:6).

What did we learn from Geronimo?

Consequently, faith comes from hearing the message, and the message is heard through the word of Christ. (Romans 10:17)

We learned that God's Word manifested in love is so powerful that it can reach anyone—even one whose culture we did not understand. The Indians on the reservation had such a different way of life that we were careful to respect them and honor this unfamiliar territory.

We are therefore Christ's ambassadors, as though God were making his appeal through us. We implore you on Christ's behalf: Be reconciled to God. (2 Corinthians 5:20)

We wanted them to see Jesus in us as we approached them in love. God's love is something every human needs, and anyone can be used by God to reach people, even those from very different cultures.

We also clearly learned that it doesn't matter how tough a child is, God can reach him. We don't have to fear, only trust in the One who is there to perform the work we cannot complete by our own devices in and of ourselves. Then the once tough child can become an ambassador of the gospel where we cannot go.

> *To the weak I became weak, to win the weak. I have become all things to all men so that by all possible means I might save some. I do all this for the sake of the gospel, that I may share in its blessings.* (1 Corinthians 9:22–23)

(We no longer have altar calls as we did the first year of camp. We are now careful not to allow accepting the Lord to be a time to receive everyone's attention. We screen each counselor to be sure that they know how to lead a child to the Lord. Accepting the Lord at camp is now a personal time with God and the camper's counselor.)

Chapter Four

Maria's Prayers

There are campers who stick out in your mind for different reasons: because of their struggles with sin, because they have remained faithful to God despite the horrendous things they've endured, or because of their incredible personalities. Maria represents all of these. She stands out because of the type of abuse she went through and how devoted she was to God and her siblings through it all.

As children, Maria, Theresa, and Juan lived with their father and mother in Texas on a farm secluded miles from other people. Maria believed her dad secluded them this way for two reasons. One, so that others couldn't hear their screams when he physically and sexually abused them, and, two, so that truant officers would not find out that they were not attending school.

"He could not stand losing control over us," Maria said, "Besides he needed us for the farm work."

Abuse was a daily affair. Their tortured minds wondered when the next episode would begin. They never knew what would set their father into an uncontrollable rage. In a craze he would grab one of their arms, twisting it behind their back just short of snapping. Often this was done in demand of a recant or other verbal submission. His untempered rage petrified the mother and the children, so they submitted to heavy labor on the farm as well as to the abuse. Maria would often offer herself instead of Theresa for the sexual abuse. This way she could protect her sister and not have to watch or hear her go through the pain.

Maria described her father as being so possessive of each of them that he wouldn't let them out of his sight. This was carried out to the point that he would not allow their mother to go to a hospital even upon knowing that she had advanced cancer in her throat. Maria said she watched her mother dying slowly at home. The large growth on her neck oozed and caused her to choke. At the very end of her life, the father finally took their mother to the hospital, but it was too late.

The children were not allowed to go, which, Maria said, hurt the most. "Why couldn't he let us be there for her at the end? I didn't even see my mother die," were her painful words. She hated her dad with a fierce anger for letting this happen. After her mother died, the father grew more violent and remained drunk most of the time until finally he felt he could not take care of his children. He gave relatives from California custody of the children.

However, they were not safe even in that home, as they again met neglect and abuse. It was not as bad as before, but they suffered with improper discipline and heart-wrenching neglect. In being disciplined, they were either put in scalding hot water in a bath tub or made to strip naked in the winter and be hosed down in the backyard. They watched as the relatives gave their own children gifts, food, and clothes, while Maria and her siblings were given leftovers and hand-me-downs. The pain of feeling worthless shut her spirit down even further.

When Maria came to camp at the age of thirteen she was unreachable. She would not let anyone near her because she was unable to trust anyone. She looked at all of us with hardened, scowling eyes and never smiled. Only God can reach special children like these. Through the worship music and the unconditional love she experienced at camp Maria softened. She accepted the Lord the second time she came to camp!

Many "God" things started to happen as Maria began praying for everything in her life. One of the most important things was that she and her sister were saved from the abuse in the relatives' home. When Maria told us about the home she was in, we notified the authorities. After investigating, they "happened" to put them in a Christian foster home. We knew this was not a coincidence, but that God was answering Maria's prayers.

Maria grew by leaps and bounds and became an encourager to many as she testified of God's faithfulness. At camp, she was often very bold and shared in front of all the campers how great God was. She would tell others of her life and how God had come in, changing the bad to good.

As she studied the Bible, prayed, and went to church, her spirit changed so dramatically and revealed the most spirited delightful girl that had been beneath all that pain. The high point of letting herself have fun came during one winter camp. She saw everyone sledding and was hesitant to join in. After a couple mild rides and coaxing, she followed suit with one of the guy campers and wildly attacked the sledding hill, going to the highest point, getting such strong running start that they ended up in the icy stream water at the bottom. She delightfully screamed as she plunged into the chilly water, causing everyone to laugh. She repeated this half a dozen times before returning to the camp house to change. The laughter and smile on her face that day spoke loudly to all of us that Maria was free to be herself.

Besides many hilarious antics that became a common part of having Maria around, she was caring. She became a jr. counselor (refer to Appendix A, "Glossary," page 113) at the age of seventeen and enjoyed giving back to new campers what she had received. She was tireless in taking care of duties. She was diligent to accomplish her chores, whether it was dishes or bathroom duty. She made every effort to be outside on her free time so that she could be with the campers. Entertaining them and making sure that they had a good time became her priorities. Her broad smile and pleasurable laugh affected everyone at camp.

When things seemed to be going so well, a tragedy occurred at their foster home. One night Theresa was going out. Maria told her, "I feel so strongly that you should not go out. Something bad is going to happen." But Theresa would not listen, and that night, she was grabbed and raped in the street.

Maria was so hysterical when her sister came crawling home that she beat her. She went berserk, hitting her so violently that Theresa was taken to the hospital. Horror filled her brain that she could do such a thing. Both of them were sent to "Orangewood," a temporary shelter, where children are returned after a "failed placement." (Refer to Appendix A, "Glossary," page 113.)

She was in utter despair over the evil of which she had been capable. When she was young, she swore she would never strike out against another person as her dad had done so often. At Orangewood she was allowed one phone call. Maria called camp. Sobbing, she explained what had happened.

She was starting to blame God, questioned if He was doing anything, and if her troubles were ever going to stop.

I said, "God isn't making any mistakes in allowing you to be taken out of the Christian foster home in which you prayed to be placed. He probably has a plan so big and wonderful that it is better and will heal you from the present and other pains. He wants to remove your guilt over what you did and anything else for which you have never asked Him to forgive you. He doesn't reject you now nor will He ever. He wants to restore your life to more than you had before. God will use this to heal you of possible future abusing. But you have to confess everything, stay still, wait, and listen. If you do, you will watch Him use even this situation."

She was disbelieving at first, but by the time we finished talking she said, "Okay, I'm going to do this totally God's way, relax and trust that He will do something. Show me how to pray for this and to ask for forgiveness."

We prayed for forgiveness. Sobs resounded over the phone. Bondage creating fear eased. "God, please take the rage away and help Maria to never rage against another person in her life. Lord, show her that you are here loving her still," I prayed. Maria learned a deeper relationship with a God who could forgive her for even violence against her sister. She held tightly to being in His presence, a place of peace and victory.

God was quick to show Maria one way He wanted to use this situation for good. Maria's roommate when she got to Orangewood was a girl named Rocksie. As they got to know each other and swapped their stories, Maria found out that Rocksie had been at Camp Alandale the previous summer. She had been the hardest camper we had in ages. She never spoke and made sure we knew she wanted nothing to do with God.

Rocksie was a beautiful, African-American girl with long hair. The whites of her eyes were all you could see of her face. Her hair covered everything else. We knew this was a sign of deep insecurity that she was covering up with a hard shell. She, like Maria, had gone through violence at the hand of her father.

Maria shared her faith and how she was going to trust God no matter what. At Orangewood, they allow a Chaplin to conduct worship services. She encouraged Rocksie to come to chapel services. There, Rocksie finally heard what God had really done for us when He sent his Son to die in our place for our all sins against God. She realized she needed God's forgiveness for all she had done and asked how to ask Jesus into her life. Maria led her in a prayer to ask God for forgiveness. Rocksie asked, "Jesus, can I be your child?"

Maria and Rocksie began to talk about God and what they had learned at camp. They talked about what all the things in their lives meant. It really hit them both hard when Maria told her, "Well, God allowed me to be sent to Orangewood just so we would be roommates! God used my pain to let me help you find Jesus."

Rocksie got so excited that she ended up earning a higher level of rank and privilege at Orangewood (for her good behavior) than even Maria had. To her amazement, Maria and her sister eventually were returned to their previous Christian foster home. She learned to be relaxed in God's arms when things turned for the worse. It was in that time that she learned to watch God work miracles as she tried not to get in the way and mess up what He was doing to fix things. But more importantly, she learned that God could use her hurt and the abuse in her life to reach the unreachable.

Maria returned to camp for many years until she graduated out of the program at the age of eighteen. One of my best memories was being with her on a camp-out we had for high schoolers. It was a pitch black night with a zillion stars shining. As we sat on a rock she poured out all the horrible events of her life. We took each burden and laid them before the Lord for Him to heal. I held her as she sobbed and shared her story. She had to work hard to free herself of all the pain. It didn't take just one night. She committed to get in God's presence with each remembered horror and give each one to God.

Maria recognized that God was the only one who had been there for her through all her horrors. Mentally she could testify that He had been the only faithful one. It took years of watching God be consistently faithful before she was convinced of His love and care enough to trust Him. But once she was convinced, she became faithful to Him in everything. She sought His direction for jobs and relationships instead of trusting her own judgement and retaining control. With her beautiful, strong voice, she expressed this with songs she sang at camp. She faithfully attended and served at her church, even singing solos there, as well.

After Maria graduated from high school she got a job, worked hard, received promotions, and decided to save enough money in order that she could get guardianship of Theresa and Juan. Her dream came true, and they lived together for several years. Maria even gave her sister a beautiful wedding, and she paid for her brother to go to junior college.

However, Satan hates those who do good, who rob him of ones he had tried to destroy. One night she ran out of gas on the freeway. When she got out of the car a man leaped from the bushes and dragged her out of view of the passing cars. He ripped at her clothes as she yelled, "No! This is not going to ever happen again!" She fought so hard and prayed. He finally gave up but stuffed her in her car trunk so he could get away. She was found in the morning, cold and tired. She had yelled all night for help because she feared that the man would come back.

Maria was horrified and confused by this ordeal. There were too many questions. She called to talk. "Is God punishing me? Why would He let this, of all things (a sexual assault), almost happen when I try so hard to follow Him completely? Doesn't He see me going to church all the time and praying? Can't He help us?"

Tough questions like this require God's hand to touch our hearts of pain, or we can brood and alienate God for years.

Carefully, I talked and prayed with her. We concluded that God did save her from being raped. The man did not come back. Satan had used Maria's forgetfulness in filling the car with gas as an opportunity to harm her and crush one of God's most potent warriors. Though his attempt failed, Satan would gain some victory if Maria chose to hold this against God. However, Maria saw the truth—God still was the only one who faithfully loved and cared for her all her life. Maria decided to put the blame where it belonged—on Satan. God is still praised by all the many more good choices Maria has made.

Looking back over her life we can see clearly that misfortunes and afflictions in Maria's life taught her perseverance, character, patience, and strength. God used all she endured for good.

Consider it pure joy, my brothers, whenever you face trials of many kinds, because you know that the testing of your faith develops perseverance. (James 1:2–3)

When I think of Maria, I think of her incredible strength and infectious laugh. She has faced so much and has gained such character for having gone through it all.

See, I have refined you, though not as silver; I have tested you in the furnace of affliction. (Isaiah 48:10)

She struggled wondering where God was in the midst of the terrible times and grew from these times of questioning. We do not get to choose what kind of things will enter our lives but we do get to choose how we respond to them. We can cooperate with God to use them for our good, the good of others, and for His glory! At camp we tell the children that "It is not what happens to you in life that determines who you are but how you respond to it." Maria chose to be devoted to God and her siblings, through it all. Now she is an example to us all.

He is like a man building a house, who dug down deep and laid the foundation on rock. When a flood came, the torrent struck that house but could not shake it, because it was well built. (Luke 6:48)

My heart is grateful that God chooses those who have been hurt like Maria for higher purposes. God enables these chosen ones with extra strength. They have been given a special purpose because of what they have gone through. Their hearts are even more motivated to caring works because they feel more deeply for others who have gone through similar pain.

Are there any in your life that God would have you lead through their pain to be useful servants of God? (Refer to Appendix D, "How to Help a Hurting Person without Getting Hurt," page 120.)

Chapter Five

Charity's Story

From the moment she arrived at her first camp, her expressionless face revealed the worst had happened to her. At the age of twelve, Charity's pained heart was wary to trust anyone. But the flooding love she received at camp from God assured her He was the answer. Jesus was real, and the truth of His love opened her heart to receive Him. She felt Him in the songs we sang. She saw Him in the beauty of the forest. And the Bible filled her heart with truth that seemed as sweet as honey.

The following year Charity returned to camp a changed girl. At campfire time, thirteen-year-old Charity decided to share her testimony. She opened by exclaiming, "I am so glad to be back at Camp Alandale!" She nearly fell out of the chair in her excitement, and several chuckled and cheered in agreement.

Then she began again, "But it is going to be hard for me to share my story. My mother, who has been a prostitute always seems to have a new guy around." She stopped this time to try to control the emotions that were boiling up.

She managed a few words here and there. She got out that her mother's boyfriend raped her while her mother was gone when she was five years old. Scared and hurt, she ran to her mother when she returned for help and told her what had happened. Her mother did not turn out to be a safe refuge for her as she did not believe her five-year-old daughter.

She received punishment for her "lie" and was dragged by her long blond hair up two flights of stairs to the attic. She was locked in the attic for five days without food and no place to rest her head. She was given water and a trash can in which to relieve herself. She felt she was going crazy dealing with the hurt and confusion of being raped and then accused of inventing a lie.

A couple years later Charity was raped again by her mother's new boyfriend. Convinced her mother would believe her this second time, she told her what had happened. However, her mother reacted the same and began to drag her up to the attic. She struggled and got her hair free and began fighting with all her might, using her fists. Her mother's strength proved too strong. She eventually found herself in the same attic with nightmares flooding her mind of what the previous stay had been like. She decided she had to find a way out. The way out was a small window near a tall tree. Miraculously, she safely made her way down the three stories on the tree's branches. Quickly she found someone to call the police, and she turned herself in to the county for protection.

This was not the end of her horror. A year later, Charity was returned to her mother where she continued to be sexually abused by relatives and strangers until the age of eleven. At that point, she was finally taken away because of her mother's involvement in drugs.

On many occasions she had witnessed her mother "high" and wondered why the drugs were more important to her than her own daughter. She asked her mother and she replied, "Here. You have some and see." It was during this time that her mother introduced her to several types of drugs.

The pain in Charity's voice was accentuated by her questions. "Isn't a mother supposed to protect and teach her child good things?"

Because she had returned to camp stronger in her faith, she was able to share her entire story at campfire. She was also able to move on from the questions to enthusiastically encourage others to accept Jesus as the One who would protect and teach them as well as heal their hurting hearts.

When an abused girl is able to believe in God despite what Satan did to crush her spirit, it gives God great glory. Satan tries to defame God's name by crushing an innocent child. But when a whipped child still sees God as the Way, it extinguishes Satan's lies.

As he went along, he saw a man blind from birth. His disciples asked him, "Rabbi, who sinned, this man or his parents, that he was born blind?" "Neither this man nor his parents sinned," said Jesus, "but this happened so that the work of God might be displayed in his life." (John 9:1–3)

Charity's parents *did* sin and that caused her a lot of pain. Others sinned against her as well. What happened to her had nothing to do with her sin. Yet, the work of God was displayed in her by all she went through for the good of others. Many children accepted the Lord that week after hearing Charity's story.

You intended to harm me, but God intended it for good to accomplish what is now being done, the saving of many lives. (Genesis 50:20)

Chapter Six

Flames of Healing

Like many spiritual experiences, I could never really give someone a complete picture of what camp is like. However, because camp is such a unique ministry we wish to try and give you a little taste of the special moments at camp. Since campfire time is the heart of the healing ministry, it seems best to paint a picture of what happens there. Most campers say campfires are their favorite time.

Campfires burst alive as campers run to find their perfect spot in the circle next to their friends and favorite counselor. A single row of fifty chairs circles a campfire ring. The fire is starting to burn with a trail of white smoke which adds to the forest scents. A wooden platform that is used as a stage for the worship leaders closes one end of the circle of chairs. The sunset sets the sky aflame, but soon we will be sitting under a dazzling sky full of stars. The fire is not close enough to warm everyone so campers bundle up and huddle together. Two chairs are vacant just off to the center of the stage that will be used later.

On the stage the musicians' guitars reflect the light of the fire. The tambourines are ready. The amplifier is turned up, and the incredible worship leaders begin with fun Christian songs that get everyone out of their seats. Hand motions, dancing, and clapping are all part of the experience. Then comes silly skits with a spiritual moral. In time, the mood changes as the worship leaders return to the stage and play slower songs to prepare everyone's hearts for the testimony time.

The two vacant chairs are now occupied. A counselor or junior counselor sets the pace for testimony time as he or she shares his or her journey to the Lord. Since many counselors are drawn to minister at Camp Alandale because they had once been abused, campers are amazed to hear what their counselors have been through and how much they have been transformed. Many junior counselors are past campers who are now serving at camp in their teen years. They share how camp has been used by God to save and heal them. Tears often roll down their cheeks from their memories. Campers see living miracles and the possibility of transformation and healing in their own lives. These examples of sharing deep hurts give the campers a pattern to follow and the boldness to share their own lives with everyone there.

So next we ask the campers if any of them would like to share. Slowly they get some courage, and a hand goes up. What comes next can be shocking. One girl may tell the story of a multiple rape by a group of boys who had a knife or gun at her head or throat. Or the story may involve a child who had multiple relatives, young and old, who were not stopped from committing incest, leaving the child feeling undefended and hopeless. He or she has no one to turn to. A story is many times accompanied by wrenching sobs of pain as a camper fights to gain composure.

The battle in other campers is evident from the quiet sobs of those who are relating to what is said. They, too, may be reliving their nightmares. One may leave the campfire as his or her counselor goes after him to counsel and console. Some of these accept the Lord while they are away from the campfire. Some receive the deep healing that their souls crave, and in time they are able to forgive their abusers. They are finally being freed of their past. Back at the campfire some have buried their heads in their counselors chests or are hiding their faces in their jackets until someone approaches them to console them.

Soon another camper is sharing his story of brutal beatings and a parent who finally abandoned him at the age of five in a hotel. Dependent on him for care are siblings who are two and three years of age, and he is scared. With food for only two days, there is guilt and the strain he experienced as he failed to change diapers properly, feed them, or keep them safe. He felt he just had to survive until their mom returned!

Finally he realized their mom was not coming back. Desperate pain filled his voice as he told his story.

They were finally discovered by someone who called the police. He went on to share the fear of being taken away in a police car, and the aching and tearing at being separated from his siblings. He never saw them again because his siblings were adopted. At this point another camper started sobbing in her seat.

Then there might be a testimony of a camper who has been to camp before who shares how Jesus has turned his life around. His story also starts with being separated from his family and put in Orangewood. (Refer to Appendix A, "Glossary," page 113.) He shares his anger and how his fight with the system led to being moved around to more than twelve foster and group homes.

Finally, he came to Camp Alandale and found God's love and healing for his heart. Now he is praying to be reunited with his family, but because dad is in jail and mom is still on drugs there seems to be little hope. "Besides," he says, "being with my family would probably just ruin my life." He shares how Jesus has helped him to accept that and to see he is better off in the system (refer to Appendix A, "Glossary," page 113) even if he thinks "it stinks to be a foster kid." Deep down though, like any child, he still naturally craves to be in his family, a real family, or any family.

By the end of the testimonies we feel a mixture of raw emotions ranging from agonized anger to incredible joy and awe. There is no way to describe the evening to anyone, as hard as we try. So much happens and cannot be put into words because it is the quiet, powerful workings of the Holy Spirit in the campers and EACH person at the campfire.

You can't even total up what happens. It doesn't cut it to say five accepted the Lord and three rededicated! It is a multiplication that happened in a spiritual dimension that is in God's realm of the infinite. For every camper that shares a story, several other campers are touched in a special way. Maybe it is a deeper understanding of how their abuse fits in their lives. Or God may perform a deep healing. Or God may clearly call them to serve Him. Mostly, they find a place where finally others understand what they have felt and gone through. It feels safe to share what others have told them to not tell. At last, someone believes them and listens with love and care, holding them and letting them know it was not their fault and that God does not hate them. They are told they did not do something to deserve this, and they are not something awful because it happened to them. They are not forever stained by their past. And the best news to many is that NO sin of theirs is too big for God to forgive.

At the same time as several campers are being impacted, so are the junior counselors, many of whom once were campers. Maybe they feel God saying for them to live more fully or differently for Him because it is so worth it to see people saved and healed. Maybe a past pain that the jr. counselor has not dealt with is opened and healed dramatically with the help of a director or counselor. These are the times when the pain is released as the past is shared.

At the last campfire of the week, we give each person a pine cone. We discuss how campers and counselors alike can cast the pain from the past into the healing flames of the campfire. As the sharp points on the pine cone tips are pricking their hands as they hold them, we explain that we have all felt hurts that need to be released so they do not continue to prick us. We suggest that each consider transferring their pain to Jesus. As songs of Jesus' love and the gift of His life are played, one by one each person comes forward when they are ready and throws their pine cone in the campfire.

Often we wonder how all the counselors and junior counselors handle the intense emotions we encounter at camp. It is only by God's grace that we can make it through each camp. One of the neat things to see is how God's work is also potent in the lives of the counselors and junior counselors as well as in the lives of the campers. After camp every year some counselors change their career focus or their academic pursuits and decide to work with children. Others feel the calling to be missionaries and bring God's message of healing and redemption all over the world. But all of the counselors say that they were changed for good and will never look at life the same. They desire to give total control of their lives to God so that He can continue to use them for such eternal purposes.

Around the campfire I often feel that deep things like this are happening, but I can't always put my finger on them. It's like seeing God's Hand at work but not knowing exactly what is happening. The awe and wonder of it all can feel paralyzing. Sometimes it is hard to break for one-on-ones (refer to Appencix A, "Glossary," page 113) after testimony times. Everyone wants to bask in the moment. Some campers and counselors gradually walk off in silence. How do you explain a whole week of camp, day after day of seeing so many souls touched and changed for God's glory? How do you explain how you feel after a whole summer of that? I cannot really put it into words that give it justice. But it seemed I should try.

(Most of the stories in this book come from campfire time when campers poured their hearts out to us. Refer to Appendix C, "Statistics of Abuse and How Camp Helps," page 117.)

Chapter Seven

Reynaldo's Testimony

Reynaldo was twenty years old the first time he shared the extent of his abuse. He presented his testimony in front of 150 camp supporters. It never entered our minds that it was so important to him to really share what camp meant to him. For him, these were the ones, who through their financial gifts, had been sending him to camp all those years.

He began by explaining that the first camp he attended was in 1987 at the age of thirteen. He shared that his first thought upon arriving at camp was, "What did I get myself into?" A flood of people with decorated baskets of snacks in their hands had converged on the arriving bus. As children piled off the bus, excitement electrified the air. Returning campers were hugging past counselors.

The scene was different from anything he had ever experienced. Everyone seemed so happy. He had never seen people so glad to see each other. He was used to the gangs in Santa Ana. He lived on a street that police had decided to ignore. Brook Street was controlled by the gangs. The heaviest drug deals were held down the street from him. Pornography and prostitution were rampant everywhere. What he was witnessing before him was confusing his perspective on life. Was it real? Could people be this happy?

When it was time to leave camp, he experienced the same sadness that the other campers were feeling. As he made a cold reality check, he felt he was just going to have to put on the old mask of toughness to survive at home. But the love at camp really affected him, causing him to question what was reality—camp or the life to which he was returning? At home, his neighborhood swallowed him up again.

The second time he returned to camp, he had a special counselor who had been a favorite of many campers over the years, Jon Farmer. Jon had a way of being able to disarm campers and gain their confidence quickly. He shared openly and frankly, was not threatened by tough exteriors, and gave unconditional love. Reynaldo fed on all of that. When Reynaldo risked quizzing Jon with, "Why do I have a life like I do?" Jon did not have to recoil. He went to Scripture and explained things clearly and honestly. Sitting on a rock, overlooking a 180-degree forest landscape, Reynaldo decided to ask Jesus to forgive him for all he had done and asked to be a child of God.

During his testimony given before the camp supporters, Reynaldo disclosed to the audience what he had endured. His sharing was intense but his God-touched heart shown through. He lived with his mother and four sisters at the time. They all had been physically abused by the father. As Reynaldo said it, "We were beat hard—as hard as in any gang fights I've seen on the streets." His father had beat them just for asking him questions or needing his help. One time, Reynaldo had caught his pant leg in a bicycle chain. When he saw he was hopelessly stuck he called from the yard for his dad whom he could see just inside the house. His father finally came out and ripped him out of the chain and took him inside. He beat Reynaldo fiercely for ending up in a situation where he was a bother to his father.

Reynaldo watched as his father attacked his mother, ripping open her back with each lash of an extension cord. He attacked the children with anything he could find. Reynaldo explained that the year before he came to camp, his mother had called the police to report his father. She found out he had been sexually abusing the older girls for years. This was too much. He had gone too far. It was the final straw. Shock hit as he and his sisters were taken to Orangewood.

He was scared by the stories the other children were telling him. Many had been in the "system" a long time and had not returned home.

As he shared with the camp supporters, "That night I cried for the first time I could remember. It may seem silly, but I missed my mother. I wondered if I would ever go home again."

Unlike the many he had met, he did not have to stay in the system, but returned to his mother within a week. His mother came to extricate them as soon as she could. But because he now had a social worker, Reynaldo qualified to come to Camp Alandale. His mother decided to send him when she found out about the camp.

At Reynaldo's second camp, he understood that as a Christian he should not continue being in a gang. He tried to explain to Jon, his counselor, that a person cannot survive in Santa Ana without being in a gang where "you protect each other." But Jon directed him with the Word of God, and at the age of fourteen he left the gang, depending on God for His faithful protection.

Reynaldo began to pray for his family. He thought, for a long time, that nothing was happening. Everyone continued fighting, but then he noticed they started to talk now and then. Gradually, they began to eat a meal or two together.

Reynaldo arranged with us for his younger sisters to attend camp. He even earned enough money to pay for most of the cost of sending them to camp. We told him that he did not have to pay since people donated gifts for them. He countered, "I want to do the right thing. To me, the right thing to do is to pay their way and not to take a hand out. If I can do this, I should." Both of his sisters eventually asked Jesus into their lives.

Then he was able to convince his mother to let him take his sisters to church. His mother soon joined them. Four years passed. His older sisters had left home by this time but he had many conversations with them about God. He could see that God really was working in his life now. It was not as slow as he had originally thought. It was just God's way of gradually bringing them around.

After Reynaldo had shared all this on stage, he came to me and said he had much more to say. There was no time left in the program, so Reynaldo decided to mail out a letter to all who attended the event and this is what he wrote:

Dear Friends of Alandale,

I would like to thank everyone who gave me such encouraging words after my testimony. This sharing really helped me face my problems and would not allow me to stuff it all inside again. I would like everyone to know that with the help of the Wood family and other close camp friends, God is helping me deal with my feelings and unresolved pain.

The evening with you was a turning point in my life. I have always had to be strong and never show my pain. But that night with the help of Karen's loving eyes I could be myself and not worry about how weak I was acting. If it is God's calling for you to be involved with camp, you will do fine. The many counselors I had, influenced my life more than I could ever explain.

I pray that God makes it possible for each of you to influence an abused child's life. You may never be told how special you have been to that child in the week you spend with them, but believe me they will remember you and who you were for years to come.

I would like to let you know that now that I have shared my testimony with you, it is making me want to have more of a relationship with my dad. I'm willing to go out if he still wants to. I was indecisive before I shared. I want you to know that even though I did not look happy that night I am very happy. There is a joy inside I couldn't express because I was nervous and tired, so I held it back.

My past is in the past because of God, and I have let go of most of my pain. Since I shared, I am happier and I don't know why. I have more energy to go at it, even at work! When I went to work someone said, "You look happy today. Why?"

I always pray for camp and thank God for camp. If anyone else is having a hard time with their past or whatever problem they have, they should face it. I used to put my abuse aside each time. When I tried to handle it by myself I got nowhere. I'm still praying to God because with Him everything is possible and it happens in time.

Sincerely,

Reynaldo

Reynaldo had been progressing and healing from his past. However, sharing his abuse with our supporters seemed to complete the process in several areas. We have seen this many times in the lives of campers. When they open up in a secure setting and get everything off their chest, they can heal. They know they won't be condemned for being honest and will be offered real answers. If they have the opportunity to say, "I think God hates me," or "I think God is unfair," then healing can begin. The more often they share in an accepting atmosphere, where God is present, the more they can put the past behind them and go on.

When they hold it in or don't have a supportive place like camp to share what has happened, they continue to feel as though they are dying inside. More and more anger builds up to the point where they no longer feel life is worth living and then decisions to sin are easy. Yes, they have social workers and psychologists who work with them but much of that help seems antiseptic to them. These people get paid to be in their lives, so often they only share as much as they feel necessary. However, counselors at Camp Alandale are volunteers. The campers quickly become aware that these counselors are there for them, not for pay. This fact helps them to be open to share. Many times campers end their stories around the campfire by saying to the fifty who are present, "This is the first time I have ever shared the whole story."

Vulnerability is so natural at camp. Over and over campers have said, as Reynaldo did, "Why are you people coming here to be with us. We are nothing. You come just to be with us? Are you crazy? And you don't get paid? I thought you were being paid big bucks to be with kids like us or else you couldn't be so happy." The unexpected dedication of counselors makes them feel safe.

Reynaldo often says camp was a place where unconditional love was given to him. He especially mentions he found real family life and "something" after which he wanted to pattern his life. Camp is a place where people talk about God's love for campers and they get to sing to God all day. It's a place where they see another child share safely without being scrutinized by staff or peers. It is a place where others, like themselves, share how they were healed of their scars.

Not only do they receive love but also encouragement and modeling of proper values. One day after Reynaldo had been coming to camp for two years, he was telling me how hard the temptations were in Santa Ana. I labored to comprehend life in his part of Santa Ana.

I asked many questions and then got truthful with him. "Reynaldo, I'm scared for you," I said. "Every boy who has come to camp from Santa Ana after being in a gang eventually fell into a major temptation. You have to prove to me that God is big enough for even Santa Ana—that there is hope no matter where you live. You have got to make it. Promise me that you won't fall." I hoped that by making himself accountable to me, and knowing how disappointed I would be if he fell, that he would think twice in a temptation. Now Reynaldo has been the first of several who have made it even though they lived in gang-ridden Santa Ana.

In 1990 we asked Reynaldo to be a junior counselor. This is when his healing really accelerated. He learned how to talk to God about his pain. It was explained to him that when we get in God's presence where we feel He is right there with us then we can ask God to touch the pain personally. We explained that it is painful work that we have to push ourselves through. However, God can reach in and take a lot of hurt in a moment if we let go. He meets us where we are, showing us what to say and do.

So, at our encouragement Reynaldo went off alone. It was a warm summer day. He sat by the pool alone. It was a place where he had many a fun afternoon with other campers. He could face the pain or hide. He could decide to press on or be trapped by his past. He chose to relive his life with God. He followed God's quiet voice and did as God said. For two hours he poured out his pain with tears flowing from his sorrow. It frightened us how long he was there just agonizing.

When he finally returned from the pool, he was radiant and buoyant. He was free and joyful. His eyes said it all. The hard, dark oppressive look was gone and was replaced by a tender look. Reynaldo was free of the tyranny of his past and his hate for his dad. He had forgiven him for everything just as we had suggested he try to do.

It was not until he shared his testimony with our supporters though, that he could bring himself to think of associating with his dad again and to even pray for him. Removing scars comes in stages where God deals with one issue after another and when God sees that we are ready. At the pool Reynaldo had found God and had allowed Him to get him to the point of forgiving his dad!

As a junior counselor Reynaldo worked hard. He wanted to give back what he had received. Now he was treating the campers like special people. He played hard with them at free times. He always had a football or basketball game going, laughing with them and putting a hand on their shoulders. He shared his testimony at campfires and held others who were crying after sharing their own testimonies.

One day when we were preparing food together he said "I want you to know I thank you for saving my life."

I mumbled, "God has done it, not me," and was walking away when he stopped me, took my shoulders and looked in my eyes to say, "You don't understand. I really want you to listen." I had never seen him act like this before, putting his hands on me. I was startled but decided to listen.

He continued, "All the friends I had when I first came to camp are either dead from knifings, overdoses, or suicide. One other is in a mental institution. Only, I, who came to this camp, am not messed up. I want you to understand. I meant you literally saved my life, and I want to thank you!"

I stared at him for a while taking in his intense look and all he was trying to say. It had never occurred to me how God thoroughly wants to save people. He does not only save them from their sins and hell but He gives them a real life, without gangs and drugs and other sins that destroy. There should be praise to God for saving a person from living the life Satan purposed them to live.

My focus had been to see campers enjoy a deep spiritual relationship with God. I wanted to know how often they had gone to church, prayed, and read their Bible. It had been all that mattered to me. I knew nothing of what it really was like to live on Brook Street. I did not know what Reynaldo endured there. It was violent and dangerous. God had seen how he lived, however, and wanted a better life for Reynaldo. Reynaldo had seen what a miracle it had been to survive where most of his other friends were dead.

What Reynaldo shared rocked my world for the next month as I let it sink in. I was amazed. Over the course of the next couple of years I often returned to ruminating thoughts of what he said. God cares about each person so much. He even focuses on each life. Then I had questions. How many campers would have also been dead or in jail if they had not come to camp? How many would have done violence to others? How many lives were saved by God's act? That in itself is much.

I should not evaluate their inability to reach the level of spiritual maturity that I want them all to have right away as empty-handed. Just because I want them all to rise to being missionaries and pastors, doesn't mean that is what God has planned for them. In essence, I am judging what God has already done in their lives as unacceptable. The reality is that God is not finished with them yet, and He is always right on track!

What if many of them remain nominal Christians all their lives but have much better lives than if they did not know God? What if they remain living in ghettos and there they are able to reach many for Christ. Even if they live in dysfunction, maybe they will relate better to neighbors and they can save many others from pain. The pressure of living with hurting people who hurt back probably would overload anyone who has not lived their life.

I soon realized that I needed to applaud their every right decision, instead of just discussing whether they went to church every Sunday. If they had made awesome decisions to not lash out or to not get into a gang or to not use drugs, it was time to get excited over them. It is a miracle that they continue to try to do the right thing when they face family strife and have no one to turn to daily. To not notice these decisions is to dismiss the praise that is worthy of God's amazing grace working in their lives daily.

All of Reynaldo's decisions were easy to applaud. He came up with so many ideas to not only make things better for himself but especially for his family. When he was sixteen years old, he found four jobs (two were paper routes) so he could save enough money to move his family off Brook Street. It only took him two years. Then he set his goal on saving enough money to buy his mother a car. She had a profession but couldn't support herself until she had a car. So this teen's first car went to his mother. When things became financially stable for the family, and he knew they would be able to provide for themselves, he finally saved for his own car.

At work he was always promoted quickly. He had a good work ethic as well as a quick mind. He did not need to be told what to do. He always saw the next thing that needed to be done and did it without prompting. As he was promoted his leadership and teaching skills were seen, and before long he was a manager at the place where he worked. While working at a fast food restaurant, an executive from the Hyatt hotels saw him working and approached him on the spot to offer him a job.

About this time we asked Reynaldo if he would like to be a camp counselor. The minimum age for a counselor is twenty-one but Reynaldo was ready at twenty. He was so attentive to his campers, taking care of their every need. He easily led them to the Lord and was able to speak to them from the experiences of his life. These spoke right into their hearts. They knew he understood whatever pain they talked about. Watching him study a camper's eyes as they talked and giving a hug at just the right time amazed us.

One day when we had a moment to talk about how camp was going I told him that he was such a natural. We were so pleased to see his ministry to the campers. I continued with, "If you keep on like this we are going to be asking you to come on staff at camp!" He said, "Really?" I emphasized that all he had to do was find the right girl to marry. He was disbelieving, but I knew I had planted a thought in his head. This felt so right.

A year later he introduced us to Maria. "What a jewel," I told him, "but she is not a Christian. What are you thinking? Haven't we taught you at camp that missionary dating is not a good idea?"

Reynaldo answered, "I know and I have long ago made up my mind not to marry a non Christian, but I am hoping to lead her to Christ." After the "mini lecture," we returned to Maria who took our breath away, too. Her humble, sweet personality did seem to match Reynaldo's so well!

We saw more of Maria, and before we knew it he had led her to the Lord. He took her to his church where she fell in love with ministry to the junior high youth group. The youth loved her. She was loving and fun. Reynaldo fell more and more in love with her. He had made sure his mother and sisters were financially stable and now he felt free to marry Maria.

He had saved and prepared for marriage, too. He was able to provide a beautiful wedding and take his bride to Hawaii for their honeymoon.

When their first baby was four months old, the camp needed to find a "Vision Promotion" person (a person who shares about camp to churches and major donors). Reynaldo so fit the job. He had no problem talking to anyone about the camp he loved. When we asked Reynaldo to consider coming on staff at camp, there was no hesitation. Before Reynaldo and Maria got married they had decided that if the Lord ever found them worthy to serve Him full time, they would say yes. What a special day it was to have a past camper who had turned from being a gang member to follow God and eventually become one of our vital staff members!

Remember how the LORD your God led you all the way in the desert these forty years, to humble you and to test you in order to know what was in your heart, whether or not you would keep his commands. (Deuteronomy 8:2)

Reynaldo has been a jewel made by God himself.

The LORD their God will save them on that day as the flock of his people. They will sparkle in his land like jewels in a crown. (Zechariah 9:16)

He had started saving to buy a home before we asked him to come on staff. He now lives in a beautifully cared for home. He has raised his support, worked hard and productively, and is growing to be a strong oak.

The Spirit of the Sovereign LORD is on me, because the LORD has anointed me to preach good news to the poor. He has sent me to bind up the broken-hearted, to proclaim freedom for the captives and release from darkness for the prisoners, to proclaim the year of the Lord's favor and the day of vengeance of our God, to comfort all who mourn, and provide for those who grieve in Zion—to bestow on them a crown of beauty instead of ashes, the oil of gladness instead of mourning, and a garment of praise instead of a spirit of despair. They will be called oaks of righteousness, a planting of the LORD for the display of his splendor. (Isaiah 61:1–3)

Reynaldo has seen his mother and all of his sisters accept the Lord as of this last year. Rey was able to love his father after he was released from jail. He shared that he had forgiven him for the abuse. Again, he assisted his father when he was being deported to Mexico. Rey shared about his faith which, he continues to pray, his father will one day embrace. The two younger sisters who first came to camp seven years ago now serve as loving and valuable jr. counselors. They also have joined a team of past campers that Reynaldo has assembled to share about camp with him in his role as Vision Promotion Director. His mother now has told the rest of his extended family about Jesus and many of them have accepted the Lord. Yes, we call them *oaks of righteousness, a planting of the LORD for the display of his splendor.* They each now wear *a garment of praise instead of a spirit of despair.*

Chapter Eight

Our "Kids" Grow Up!

One of our greatest delights is seeing the children, whom Satan has broken, shine for God's glory. To come full circle and see how God restores a life is breathtaking. We have had the unique privilege of becoming a family for our campers. We become so close in time spent together and are blessed to see them accomplish God-ordained feats.

Michelle came to camp when she was nine years old. Reynaldo came when he was thirteen. Michelle made a decision to follow Jesus when she was young but really did not fully give her life for God's use until she was fifteen. Reynaldo fully realized his need to give his life completely to God at fifteen also. Michelle walked away from an involvement in Satanism. Reynaldo walked away from gangs. Each life was in the balance. They could have gone either way, but each stayed close to Jesus because of camp involvement in those teen years and learned the truths that set them on the "Rock."

Both went on to serve at camp as junior counselors. They were wonderful junior counselors, giving sacrificially to the campers in the same way in which they were served. When the adult counselors were worn out and tired, Reynaldo and Michelle were still at the campers' sides playing with them. At campfire, Reynaldo would share with campers about his experience of abuse. Visibly he shook, but he told his story to encourage them of God's love and faithfulness and what He now meant to him. And each time Reynaldo shared, God healed more of his heart.

Because of their maturity, we started Reynaldo and Michelle as counselors early, at twenty years of age. Our minimum age is normally twenty-one but we felt they were ready. Campers felt a heart of compassion from each of these who understood where they, the campers, were coming from. Watching their warm glowing looks as they gazed into campers' faces and their tender, consoling arms placed around the campers' shoulders caused us to take notice. How did they grow to be so loving when they had not received this kind of love at home?

Each of them led a special person to the Lord, people whom they would each end up marrying. Michelle was an incredible evangelist and would regularly go climbing with a group of friends. She would often share the Lord with the whole group, but one of the friend's finally started asking questions, and she eventually led him in the sinner's prayer.

Reynaldo noticed a girl who was really special, but she was not a Christian. Reynaldo started sharing the Lord with her and with a soft heart she began responding to God's voice in her life. When Michelle announced her engagement to Angus, and Reynaldo announced his to Maria, we expressed our willingness to do their marriage counseling. We were so blessed! In the pleasure of doing their marriage counseling with both couples, we were delighted to see how wonderfully matched they each were for each other. This was the first time for us to do marriage counseling and it was for two of our camper "kids."

I offered to make Michelle's wedding dress and then volunteered Robin to do the wedding ceremony. Michelle had asked Robin to do her mother's grave side memorial three years earlier. It was Robin's first time to officiate a memorial and now this would be his first wedding. It was a beautiful wedding. Flowers flooded the church with fragrance. One of our counselors who had known Michelle for twelve years, arranged at least fifty bouquets. She was a radiant bride, as was Maria for Reynaldo. Reynaldo's love and respect for Maria showed she was a woman worthy to be sought after. The looks in their eyes for each other were genuine, attending to each other as no other.

We are so very proud of these two campers who have found God's partners in God's way and plan to serve Him with their lives! We are also fascinated by the way God uses the pain inflicted on children for their ultimate good.

See, I have refined you, though not as silver; I have tested you in the furnace of affliction. (Isaiah 48:10)

God carefully stripped Reynaldo and Michelle of a worldly view. They had God's ways modeled before them at camp when their own families' lives were a wreck. They used their pain to learn perseverance, patience, and strength. They purposed to live life differently than their parents had.

He is like a man building a house, who dug down deep and laid the foundation on rock. When a flood came, the torrent struck that house but could not shake it, because it was well built. (Luke 6:48)

Chapter Nine

Ti's Anchor

Ti grew up in Vietnam where his family lived in poverty. His father wanted to escape from this destitute life to the possibility of a better life in America. Out of Ti's family, his father favored only Ti's older brother. He never told the family of his plan to escape. He wished only to bring his favorite son and himself to America. The cost was high, but his father put together the money and paid the smugglers who promised passage to America and to freedom.

Secrecy was required, so the smugglers did not tell Ti's father the day or the time they would leave. When the day came, his favorite son was nowhere to be found. Hurried by the smugglers, the father had to leave on the spot. Ti was the only one at the house. His father forced Ti to go with him because he did not want to waste the money he had paid for two passengers. Ti was only five years old when this took place.

As "boat people," they suffered unmentionable things that caused Ti intense grief. With downcast eyes, he would not say much, but he did express that he saw half the people around him die on this journey to freedom. The boat was so crowded that often they thought it would capsize. No food was provided. Starvation caused the passengers to violently descend on each other and steal what was available.

In America, Ti's father became an alcoholic and when enraged beat Ti for many years. They moved often across the country and back. Ti rarely went to school. He was a slave to his father until one day when the abuse was reported. He was taken into custody by the Orange County Social Services (refer to Appendix A, "Glossary," page 113) where he was put into a foster home.

A year had passed since he had been taken from his abusive and neglectful father when he came to Camp Alandale at the age of thirteen. After enduring this abuse, Ti was a mixture of pain, fear, and rage. At his first camp he was uneasy around so many non-Asian people. Counselors are chosen randomly for the campers by a computer program. His counselor at camp turned out to also be Asian, which helped with his uneasiness. The counselor also had a good knowledge of Buddhism which happened to be Ti's religious upbringing. This counselor gloriously led Ti to the Lord. Jesus made Himself so real to Ti at his first camp that he could not resist Him. Ti's heart jumped with joy as he felt real love, God's pure love for the first time.

One year later after Ti had been to his second camp, God's Spirit drove him to read through the entire Bible that he won as a camp award. Ti was unable to put it down. He read it from cover to cover in about two weeks. This happened again the next year after his third camp. He was driven to read through the entire Bible again. The amazing thing was that he hardly knew how to read. He could hardly pull himself away to eat or to provide personal care. Ti expressed that God taught him words as he was obedient to God's Spirit drawing him to learn. In disbelief, I picked up a Bible and pointed to the word redemption and asked him to read it. He said, "That word is redemption and it means God let Jesus die to save us." He said, "I learned to read English from the Spirit of God." In learning to read by God's spirit, Ti found an anchor for his life, a boat that would not sink, and a Father who would not abuse him.

Two years later, Ti became a junior counselor. He was a teenager who showed maturity in his faith and a desire to serve at what he called, "His beloved camp," and "home." He relished giving back to others, who were hurting, what he had been given.

From time to time, however, his pain still buried inside would surface and erupt in anger. Over the years, Ti always had a lot of guidance and support from counselors and from God's gentle hand of healing. Nevertheless, the Navy was where God taught Ti to deal with his anger. In a situation that his camp friends all feared would break him, Ti was finally healed by depending on God's constant help. It is always a surprise to see what God will use to refine us. God used many people, circumstances, and time to heal Ti.

Through the years, the pain and the anger have left. God has produced a whole person, who is able to stand up even in the military. He was even recognized for his Christianity and voted to be Religious Petty Officer.

Here is one of the many letters we received from Ti while he was in the Navy.

April 24, 1993
Dear Friends,

I hope God had blessed you as He has blessed me. The time that I have spent away from you has helped me to grow stronger with the Lord. When I was a kid you helped me by sharing His love and His word to me but as I grew older I began to depend on you to help me. And now I see why God has put me in the Navy and so far from home. Here on the ship I learn each day to grow in the grace of God day by day. My relationship with the Lord have grown to be something special, and I know when I see you again we rejoice in God's love for our lives.

Here each time I fall He speaks to my heart, and I know that He is there for me. Well that is what I want to share with you about our mighty and wonderful God. So I want to take the time to say thank you for taking the time to teach me His love. I pray that God always blesses you.

Never stopping to serve God that is the family I know and continue to be glad to know. Hope you received the other three letters from me already. I love to write and it shows. Well God always will continue to be by your side and unite you as a family.

Peace and love,

Ti

At the age of twenty-one, Ti visited his homeland of Vietnam and was reunited with his family for the first time since he was five. He led his sister to the Lord and found her a good church before he left. He used the finances provided by the military for his education to study to be able to minister to his people. He eventually brought his entire family over here where they all attend a Vietnamese church. Ti plans to one day be a pastor.

I once told Ti, "You can be a leader. God has called you for something special." When I said those words to him years ago, he thought I was wrong and could not accept those thoughts. But now he knows and believes that God is calling him to something special. Praise God!!!

In that day they will say, "Surely this is our God; we trusted in him, and he saved us. This is the LORD, we trusted in him; let us rejoice and be glad in his salvation." (Isaiah 25:9)

When we read the letters from campers, like the one above, we are humbled with awe and sparked with joy at how much God impacts their lives. Yet, the desire to reach more children, in more counties and states, wells up. The desire to be more intensely involved with God's workings and direction can be overwhelming. Living for Him is so dynamic, and the eternal ramifications are so sweeping. Half a world away people are eternally impacted!

They were hungry and thirsty, and their lives ebbed away. Then they cried out to the LORD in their trouble, and he delivered them from their distress. Let them give thanks to the LORD for his unfailing love and his wonderful deeds for men. (Psalm 107:5, 6, 8)

Ti suffered so much; yet, it eventually brought salvation to his family. The pain is worth it to Ti now since he sees it as a blessing in disguise. Ti knows being taken to a foreign country has been used to save his family.

For you, O God, tested us; you refined us like silver. (Psalm 66:10)

Chapter Ten

We Get Letters

The following are actual camper letters. They have not been edited and are just as they wrote them. Letters have always been an amazing gift of campers to us. We know it takes a lot for them to sit down, get a letter written, find a stamp, and get it mailed. Most abused children have had their education interrupted. Most have not been able to concentrate on studies when their minds are filled with concerns about what will happen next in their lives. So letters are special gifts from them, reaching out to us. We always make sure we respond to every camper letter.

To Karen,

    Thank you for giving me a hug. I was crying. I hope you have a nice Easter. When I was going down the hill I heard God say that the Woods love me and I love the Woods to. I hope I get to come back in the summer. Well I have to go bye.

Timmy

    P.S. Write back soon. Send me the paper inviting me back soon. God Bless You.

    Precious Timmy! He first came to camp at twelve years of age, in 1991. The first time he left camp he hung half his body out the bus window with arms grabbing at the air. He called out through sobs, "Don't make me go back!"

    All we could do was lower our heads and cry, too! For the first few years he cried almost all the way home on the bus, burying his face in a pillow or completely covering his head with his shirt, his body trembling.

    He was from a severely broken background, so for him, camp means a real place where he had people who loved him. It's home to him. He has settled in his heart that he had a place from now on that he could call home. Many times he went to God on his own to give Him all his past hurts since he heard how to do that at a campfire.

He is so alive when he is close to God. But He allows the pain of his past to keep him from trusting God completely. He is easily pulled into sin by the attraction of receiving love or popularity. When he gets burned he easily runs back to God. We pray for Tim (now age twenty-three) to remain in God's pure, safe love.

Dear Robin, Karen, Crystal, Jessica, and David,
(That's everybody!)
Hi! what's going on? Not much here. I really miss camp and I can't wait to come back next summer. I meet a lot of people and you guys were so easy to talk to and even easier to get close to. Camp went so fast and it was all fun. I liked it when we sang the most and at night at campfire. I didn't even want to leave. Nichelle my foster sister, and I both say all the time that we wish we were still at camp. I think it was the best time I ever had.

I really got a lot out of it. I really miss . . . well I can't say just one thing because I miss everything. I think I really learned a lot about God. I wish I could just live up there with you guys. I felt like I was at home with you guy. I never once felt out of place. Well I have to go eat.

Love lots,
Tammie

A letter from Tammie as an adult:

Karen and Robin and Family,
You guys made a helpless child see the good inside. You also taught me how to look at a person and see the inside her. You showed me love and how to give love.

I love you guys and thank God for people like you guys. You have touched my life in a very special way. I thank you guys for everything you ever did for me.

Love,
Tammie

Tammie came to camp at the age of thirteen, broken by a heart of pain. She had a very tender spirit which made her abuse all the more painful. Her beautiful body walked cautiously, with her pretty eyes almost waiting for you to look at her with evil intent. Her mother, who was a prostitute, allowed several men to sexually abuse her. A gang rape and abandonment by her mother sealed her heart in a prison. We were so amazed when she was so easily reached by God's love.

She is now a lovely mother and wife who loves the Lord.

We also get letters from counselors who volunteer their time for the campers:

To Karen and Robin,

Today is Monday March 30,1993. I wanted to say thank you for your courage in doing your ministry. And thank you because it has helped me personally to grow and to recover from so much that I had been corrupted with.

Camp Alandale is for me a bandage and repair situation. I love the way you both demonstrate love. I love the way you both demonstrate patience. I love the way you both demonstrate courteous discipline.

So overwhelmed was I during this camp that I had to turn to Robin and say "I love you." It didn't matter if he wondered why I would say it. I needed to express what I felt.

I even grow when I notice you, Robin, becoming upset over something with someone whom you love and in the next moment show love to that person. That human side helps me so much - I appreciate it all.

> Nothing can defeat love,
> Mark Leach

P.S. I'm sure Karen gets mad sometimes too. Bye you guys.

Here are some more touching letters:

Dear Robin and Karen,

You have really been a good influence on me. I really appreciate your caring hearts. I can't but feel the love of God flowing from you to all the kids. I love you!

> Love,
> Judy

Dear Mom,

Hi! How are you? I am okey. How is Dad doing? I really miss you and camp. I was really sad when I came home from camp. Did you see the lightening on Friday that we came from camp. My sister was scared. I was scared because my brother was going to church but I prayed. Everything was fine after that. How is your summer? My summer is kind of boring but when I read the Bible I fell much better because I know God is with me. When is winter camp?

> Love,
> Angie

Robin and Karen,

What's up? I miss you both! I'm going to be moving out in five weeks. Someday I would like to visit you! I've signed up for college! I'm going to Golden West Jr. College. During spring break I went with my youth group to Mexico on a mission's trip. For one week we taught the kids bout God. I saw some kids that were so poor that they couldn't afford shoes or running water. Missions trips are fun. I'm planning to go back next year. I miss you, but I got to go. Enclosed is a picture of me and one of the kids in Mexico.

Love lots,
Charlotte

Dear Karen and Robin,

How are you guys doing? Well I am doing fine. Well we are going to winter camp and I think that will be fun. Well I try to call you guys but I can't because it is long distance. Well I miss going to camp. Well now I pray and I read the Bible and I think that is new for me because now I am learning new about God. Well in school I am doing good and keeping my grades up and I am happy. Well I miss you guys because I miss talking with you. Well Karen thanks for being there for me and it was nice talking with you. Well I am so glad I got to meet with you. Well I got to go and hope to hear from you again. Bye God bless you. Jesus loves you, I love you guys.

Cindy

Chapter Eleven

Brother and Sister Reconciled

When God acts on our behalf and we see it, it is too wonderful and over-whelming to contain. Do you know the feeling? I am talking about those times when it could only have been God who performed the impossible. God is faithful to bring to completion every good work that He begins. He does not stop half way. This has been evident to us at camp in the healing that He offers to the abused. Seeing the tangible evidence of God's faithful-ness in the lives of abused children has helped us to realize that we can trust Him completely.

Innumerable camper stories testify to God's faithfulness, but one that speaks of God completing what He has begun is the story of Jane and Bill. As brother and sister they had gone through many horrors together. The abuse from parents who were on drugs was compounded by severe neglect. The pain from their parents lack of showing love was augmented by cru-elty. Brother and sister had to watch each other be beaten. When they did try to come to the other's rescue, they were thrown around like rag dolls. Stealing was their only source of food, and dirty rags were the only clothes they had to wear even for school.

When they were finally taken from their parents they were fortunate to be placed in foster homes together. However, the abuse did not stop with their parents. It continued in two of the foster homes as well. Jane and Bill first came to camp when they were living in one of these abusive homes, but did not seek our help. At camp they were full of skepticism and fiery outbursts. They were angry to hear that God was good. This concept was so foreign to their thinking! It made them even more short-tempered with us.

At our counselor prayer and share time each afternoon, Bill and Jane's counselors were able to connect on the fact that the campers were siblings and alert the rest of the counselors to their need for help. Their patience was growing thin as the counselors felt disheartened. As we prayed for direction each day, we saw breakthroughs in Bill and Jane's behavior, but their hard hearts still showed on their faces.

We were amazed when they tried to tell of their torturous past during campfire time. Jane went first. She just sat in the seat provided for an intense minute. She looked around and up to the sky and down again. Finally as she began to speak, she hid her face in her hands and began sobbing. Jane let her long brown hair fall into her face as she looked down at the ground. Her hair became wet and tangled in her face from her constant wrestling with it as she talked. Jane poured out her soul, her hair showing a picture of her anguish. Bill followed his sister with more details and affirmation of what his sister had revealed. Being a boy he felt compelled to keep his composure. He stiffly shuffled in his seat and wrung his hands. He stopped often in silence and obvious distress as he restored control over his emotions. Deep breaths, sighs, and correcting a cracking voice showed his pain.

As difficult as it was to share, the acceptance and love that followed by all the counselors and other campers began to soften them. Over three-quarters of the campers accept the Lord at their first camp. However it was after three years of coming to camp until we saw both Jane and Bill finally accept the Lord during the summer of 2000. On their return the summer of 2001, Bill was still hardened. We were so blessed to see the growth demonstrated by the peace and care flowing out of Jane though. Church attendance and a prayer life had changed her.

As the week progressed, she felt the need to share at campfire time again. She felt compelled to share the whole story along with recent events. The day before she was to tell her testimony, she was visibly in anguish. She mentioned that she was struggling trying to decide what to include and what to leave out so that her brother would not know some of her untold pain. I had no idea the depth of her struggle but suggested that we should pray about it. "Should I share it all?" she prayed.

When it came time to share, her whole story just came tumbling out, nothing stayed hidden. Camp is one of the only places most of these children feel safe enough to share. Campers come desperately hoping someone will open them up and be free them from their burdens. With Jane, her story revealed that she knew her brother was very upset with her and had been for a year now.

Bill riveted his gaze on his sister. He had treasured their last foster home, and he knew that something she had said had forced them to leave. Because of this, Bill had treated her badly all year. He did not know what had happened, but he knew that he liked the nice home in a wealthy South Orange County area. It had a swimming pool, and he had lots of friends at school and in the neighborhood.

Now the truth came out. The foster dad had been spying on Jane from a vent while she took her showers. He had started to act inappropriately towards her, and she put her foot down. This had happened in a previous foster home, and she was not going to let it happen again. Jane was moved to action when she noticed the other foster girl receiving the same treatment. She was afraid for herself and her friend. So she told the authorities.

Bill had never been told why they had to move, so he yelled at Jane for ruining the best foster home he had ever had. He was also upset because they were going to be sent to different foster homes and would rarely see each other. Jane felt she could say nothing because it was all so shameful. After their separation, they were allowed occasional visits with each other. Bill would treat his sister harshly, so she had never confided in him.

Bill was leaning forward to hear, flabbergasted at the truth. He dropped his head into his hands and shook. We were all watching to see how the truth would change their relationship, but after campfire it seemed nothing changed between them. They continued to avoid each other.

As was mentioned, they lived in different homes and rarely saw each other. So it was merely a "coincidence" that they both came to camp the same week. We could see the sovereignty of God as He directed these little details. A couple of days after Jane shared her testimony, Bill raised his hand at campfire to come up and share. With tears he shared how he had seen the foster dad sometimes go up to the attic when the girls were in the shower. Bill had been curious what was up there. So one day when he was alone, Bill climbed the ladder. To his confusion, he only found a box placed over the vent to the shower. He wondered about it, but said nothing. He was ashamed of his lack of action.

After Bill shared, his sister came up to him. Reaching out her arms, they held each other and wept at length. Then they talked and talked, making covenants of care and devotion to each other. God was bringing about reconciliation through the revealing of the truth. Bill was healed completely of his bitterness toward his sister and toward God. Jane learned that God can fix impossible things, and her questioning of God concerning this and other situations of their lives was settled more. (Truth and healing from past abuse often come in stages).

The timing of everything and the truthfulness they shared were a testament of God's perfect guidance at the right place and time. Because it is so shameful, most of the time the revelation of sexual abuse stays hidden. For their sakes, the painful situation was cleared up. Jane and Bill renewed their relationship in truth. Bill found freedom from his guilt and the ability to draw close to his sister and to God. God's grace was healing them from their past. In Christ, they found intimacy, truth, and freedom! They both vowed to never let abuse go unreported, no matter what. (Refer to Appendix E, "How to Report Abuse," page 126.) To see brother and sister reconciled was a surprise and a delight to all of us at camp.

He is the Rock, his works are perfect, and all his ways are just. A faithful God who does no wrong, upright and just is he. (Deuteronomy 32:4)

Over and over God has shown us that He can be trusted to produce good even in impossible situations. He goes beyond what we could imagine He is able to do and He completes the job, dotting the i's and crossing the t's. We all learn from Jane and Bill's reconciliation that finding the strength to tell the truth is freedom from the bondage in which Satan delights to keep us locked.

Then you will know the truth, and the truth will set you free. (John 8:32)

How wonderful it is to know a God who is able to do all these things in perfect sequence and timing!!!

Chapter Twelve

God's Faithfulness to Jenny

From the age of two until she was nine, Jenny had been sexually abused by her father who was involved in satanic rituals. Held by knife and gunpoint at times, she was too terrified to tell anyone and, thus, suffered silently for years.

Then it slipped out. A friend of hers was getting the idea that awful things were happening at Jenny's home. The friend's mother hired detectives in order to prove to the police what was going on.

When it seemed that the police were going to be slow to act, Jenny's mother fled for freedom across the country to California with her two daughters. In the process, they all found the Lord and attended a great church. Jenny started coming to Camp Alandale regularly at about that time and grew strong in her commitment to serve God.

During her teenage years, financial problems struck the family, and Jenny was sent to her maternal grandparents' home in Texas. At that home, her grandfather sexually abused her, and once again Jenny was dealing with pain she was so familiar with from her past. Disheartened yet determined not to again endure such treatment, she hitchhiked home traveling halfway across the country.

Once at home, her mother did not believe her account of Jenny's grandfather's abusive behavior. Her mother thought Jenny fabricated the story as an excuse to return home. Jenny was hurt deeply by her mother's disbelief. It was during this difficult time that we invited Jenny to be a junior counselor. All junior counselor's receive two weekends at camp in training to prepare for serving the campers' needs. During the training, God was working in Jenny's heart. During the last hour of camp, Jenny sobbed as she shared with fellow junior counselors, counselors, and staff what had happened while staying with her grandfather. She asked, "Why didn't God protect me if I'm His child?"

The next half hour we comforted Jenny. Another junior counselor, who had gone through a similar experience, joined me in ministering to Jenny's needs. We had only just begun, however, when the bus arrived to take the junior counselors home. Fortunately, a short time later, we receive permission to have Jenny stay with us for a week. Together we read through the book of Job and talked practically day and night.

The following week, Jenny served as a junior counselor at camp. She knew the campers' hurts intimately, and as she gave her testimony at the campfire, she powerfully impacted the camper's hearts. She had seen God heal her and answer her questions. Now she saw God could also give purpose to her pain: to minister to others in pain. Jenny was strong in the Lord again.

Six months later, Satan gave her another crushing blow. She found out that a deacon at her church was sexually abusing her younger sister. The family was devastated when the congregation did not believe them, and in shame, her family left the church.

Many counselors at camp continued to pray and keep in contact with Jenny. They took her to church and concerts. After a year, God's love was finally reaching her again. She needed to work through everything. But what really reached her was seeing God everywhere she went involved with the everyday things in her life and in the lives of others. Maybe it was ugly and felt unjust that her sister was molested, but God did not change. He was always there.

About that time a song spoke to what Jenny was feeling. No other had been faithful but God; not even family or church. God enabled Jenny to relate this love that God was pouring out through a song entitled "Everywhere I Go I See Your Face." Many times at camp she blessed us by beautifully singing this song and would speak of His faithfulness in showing His face to her wherever she went. She convincingly shared how everyone needed God. As an adult, she has continued in her faith.

What is the answer to Jenny's question, "Why didn't God protect me If I'm His child?" This is a question that takes years of humbly laying it before God to receive a satisfying answer.

I have told you these things, so that in me you may have peace. In this world you will have trouble. But take heart! I have overcome the world. (John 16:33)

Since we live in a fallen world, pain and injustice is really the norm. Suffering is not something strange, as our pampered culture believes. Reading through Scripture, especially the Psalms, reveals the view that life is painful and unjust. But God brings us through the pain and injustice to bring Himself glory and work for our eventual good, even if that good does not appear until eternity.

Lord, Take Care of Me!

Dear friends, do not be surprised at the painful trial you are suffering, as though something strange were happening to you. But rejoice that you participate in the sufferings of Christ, so that you may be overjoyed when his glory is revealed. (1 Peter 4:12–13)

Chapter Thirteen

From Foe to Friend

Jonathon was only four years old when the courts decided that his mother was unfit to care for her children. The verdict placed Jonathon along with his infant siblings in his father's custody. However, shortly after the adjustment, his mother kidnapped Jonathon with his younger brother and sister. Tied up, with duck tape over his mouth, she put Jonathon in the trunk of her car and fled. He traveled half way across the United States either in this state of captivity or locked in a hotel closet. The only freedom his mother allowed him was to eat or to use the restroom. Even when they reached their destination in California, his mother still forced Jonathon to live in confinement since she feared he would tell someone of the kidnapping. She was not concerned with her younger children because they were too young to speak or even to know what was happening.

They continued to move from one city to another until his mother got tired of caring for her children and abandoned them. Jonathon was eight years old. His mother's disappearance did not immediately concern him since she had left them alone for extended periods of time in the past. These times had taught Jonathon how to take care of his brother and sister. But days stretched into weeks of stealing everything "his family" needed and avoiding adults and authorities.

Ultimately, they were discovered and the family he had cared for was broken apart never to be rejoined. Because of his bitterness, Jonathon became capable of violence with a knife or his own fists. No one wanted to deal with his attitude so he was moved thirty times in two years. His reputation spread, and he soon became known to everyone in juvenile authority.

God was working in his life through all of this though, and two weeks before he came to Camp Alandale, Jonathon was allowed to room with a boy who had just been to Camp Alandale. This boy shared the Lord with his angry roommate, and a tender presence surrounded the lost boy. It was a sweet presence that Jonathon knew and vividly remembered feeling before.

As he thought about it, Jonathon realized this peaceful presence was what he had felt when he was crying in the trunk of his mother's car. He was so excited to find out who had been with him through the many trials that his young life had endured. He eagerly accepted Jesus. His newfound faith warmed him because now he knew that the person who had never left him alone in the trunk would always be with him.

The glow and excitement of that revelation were still alive when Jonathon arrived at camp. Camp was a time prepared by God for Jonathon to grow in his understanding of his new faith. He shared about his past, and God freed him from his pain. In his excitement, he asked hundreds of questions about God. His life was a testimony to the other campers that God not only can and does radically change lives, but that He is with us from the beginning. Two weeks before he had been known as someone to be feared; now, he had everyone at camp wanting to be his friend!

Jonathon only came to camp a couple more times where he continued to shine God's light and to be a witness to many. His heart of servanthood blossomed from the years of care he gave his brother and sister.

When my father and mother forsake me, then the Lord will take care of me. (Psalm 27:10 NKJV)

As you read all these stories, are you feeling God call you to help someone you know who is struggling with past pain? Appendix D, on page 120, is a good section to read. It is entitled "How to Help a Hurting Person Without Getting Hurt." It shares tips on how to help needy people who tend to put you in a parasitical relationship with them.

From Jonathon's story, believers can know even more assuredly than before that God has a special place of care for hurting children who come to camp. God cares for them and tenderly brings them to Himself. He never has nor will He ever abandon them.

. . . I will be with you; I will never leave you nor forsake you. (Joshua 1:5)

Chapter Fourteen

The Power of Prayer

When Josie stepped off the bus at her first camp, I could see that she was harboring pain deep within her heart. She spent the whole eight days of camp shutting out everyone at camp. She never wanted to talk to her counselor or to cooperate with the program.

When Josie did speak, she defied her need for God by declaring she did not even believe in Him. She boasted about joining a gang. The initiation was to take place the Thursday after she got home from camp. Her determination to join the gang had helped her to shut out everything at camp.

Anne Moore, a member of our Board of Directors, was Josie's counselor. She was deeply concerned by Josie's unresponsive attitude. Anne is the mother of five who has been a missionary with Wycliffe Bible Translators since 1972. She had traveled around the world, being in all kinds of situations. In addition to this, Anne had the Spirit of God to lead her, and three people constantly praying for her. Anne is a woman of tender and caring ways, which added to her ability to speak the truth clearly in love. She had given Josie reasons from God's Word for the painful circumstances that Josie had suffered. But still Josie did not respond.

Counselor prayer and share time is held once each day of camp. During this session, the campers have a science project or watch a video. Meanwhile, the counselors spend an hour discussing issues and praying for each child and issue. Josie's attitudes were discussed and prayed for daily.

Eight days after arriving, Josie got on the bus to leave without saying good-bye to anyone. When her counselor saw this and approached her, Josie turned away. It seemed as if the love and concern of the counselors as well as God's presence had not penetrated the thick walls around her heart.

The day after this camp ended, we were asked to speak to a group of Christians about the program. We told them wonderful stories of God's hand working in campers' lives but added the need to pray for this lost girl who wanted to join a gang. Two days later, Anne received a letter from Josie. She asked if Anne could tell her how to accept the Lord. Josie said she had done it as best as she could, but she wanted to see Anne.

Anne was ecstatic! She called Josie immediately and had Josie over to bake cookies. This was a miracle time as Anne explained that we are all sinners. We have all lied, cheated, or not helped someone when we should have. But God sent Jesus to pay the death penalty for us by dying in our place. Now all we have to do is ask Jesus to forgive us, and we become God's children. Josie had prayed something like that based on what she had heard at camp, but repeated it again with Anne. She has since found a local church and youth group to get involved with!

The miracles continued as Josie opened herself up to God. Two weeks after Josie came to camp, her roommate Desi came to camp. This girl turned out to be just as hard as Josie toward the things of God. She especially was frustrated by knowing we believed that God says sex is to be saved for marriage. Desi shared of torturous abuse and bitterness towards her abusers and the world in general. Worse yet, since she had signed up late for camp, our prayer partners had not received her name. We didn't have anyone praying for Desi. We discovered this four days into the six-day camp.

When I called our Prayer Partner Coordinator to ask for special prayer for Desi, she enlisted several people whom she called immediately. The very next day a radical change came over Desi. Her hard exterior melted away and she gloriously came to the Lord that night! Her abrasive attitude gave way to softness as she asked many questions about God. She was truly seeking understanding. After this, Josie and Desi were able to help each other in their new walk with the Lord.

Since Josie came to camp, we have gradually added more churches to pray for each camper and counselor by name while they are at camp. At present, we have twenty-six Southern California churches participating in our prayer ministry. Half of them are asked to pray the week before and the week during camp. The other half start their two weeks of prayer one week later than the first group of churches. We mail a packet of cards to each church with the first name of each camper and counselor individually printed on each card.

Since we started this intense prayer ministry, we have seen the campers become more spiritually open, more hungry for the Bible, and most amazingly they seem more ready to make hard choices to overcome problem areas in their lives. Many of the typical relational problems with the campers have greatly decreased. This aids in increased results. The miracles increase and abound with each additional set of prayer partners we have added. Moreover, we see more consistent growth and healing in campers as they return each year.

The Power of Prayer

We also send out a list of prayer requests to over 700 prayer volunteers every two months. It is obvious that the campers remain much more stable and dedicated to serving and following God than we have ever seen before. Staying on the same path over a longer period of time is usually harder for abused children, but we see more and more of it. The only thing that is different from the past is more prayer, consistently laid before God on their behalf. We have been made aware that those who have been abused need more people praying for them to break down the strongholds of Satan and to keep Satan from blinding them.

Because of the Lord's great love we are not consumed, for his compassions never fail. (Lamentations 3:22)

God delights in releasing His power through our participation. It makes me wonder, "How many people praying does it take to release the full power of God to free these children from the snare of the enemy?" Do you want to be a part? Contact us through the information listed at the end of the book in Appendix B, "How to Contact Us or Get Involved," page 114.

Good and upright is the LORD; therefore he instructs sinners in his ways. (Psalm 25:8)

Chapter Fifteen

Joanne, God's Ambassador

I turned around when I heard the deep groan of pain from a male counselor. He was holding his shin, jumping on one leg, after just being kicked by a girl named Joanne. Joanne's first camp experience was at the age of eight. She was always full of energy, running around, yet very cautious.

Now, after coming to camp for a couple of years, she started testing if the love the counselors showed her was indeed real. Joanne had it out for the men especially. This male counselor was one of her favorite victims, and he already had a couple bruises to prove it. He was patient, but this time he let her know he did not like it. Joanne just laughed and ran off. It was a laugh that said, "I am safe. He will not strike back."

Joanne did not reveal how horrible her past was until she was sixteen. She finally shared, "My dad hit my mom sometimes, and they fought all the time. We never had money for food, and we always ran to my grandmother's house for food and shelter. My dad and mom got divorced when I was five, and my mother was an okay mother until I was six and a half. She began to use drugs around that time." The drugs led her mother to not be around much to care for Joanne and her brother. Joanne was shuffled back and forth between parents. Joanne said, "My brother never lived with my mom and me. He always lived with my dad. They made us choose between them."

At the age of seven, Joanne realized she was an unwanted child when her mother gave their father custody of the children in exchange for drug money. Joanne vividly remembers, "I moved in with my dad and my dad's mother, and my dad began to physically abuse my brother and me, and he sexually abused me. When I was eight years old, I told a friend about the abuse, and we were taken away and put in Orangewood Children's Home. Then we moved in with my grandmother. After that, the courts let my mom have custody again. That's when she started going to jail and taking drugs and living with abusive men. Then after almost a year of that, my grandmother came and took us from her. I had already started going to camp."

Joanne felt fortunate that her grandmother discovered the abuse and went through the difficult court proceedings to receive custody of her and her brother. But walls were being built up around this child as she walked through these trials that seemed to surround and envelop her.

The first time Joanne came to camp at the age of eight, she was cold and reserved. During one-on-one times, Joanne stared her counselor down and refused to show any sign of response. In her mind, she did not know this person and was not about to share a thing with her. Joanne thinks it interesting that she never, in the course of her life at camp, saw her first counselor come back to camp.

Her mother was in and out of jail and in and out of her life during Joanne's first years at camp. Joanne was very angry at her mother and felt she could not trust her. This ate away at her very heart. She recalls, "My mother got off drugs when I was in eighth grade. That is when she left my brother and me and moved to Oklahoma for four years." This was the final abandonment, and Joanne sealed her heart to secure it from being hurt again by her mother.

Joanne continued to return to camp for six years but put up a tough exterior to keep others from getting too close. Yet we saw her bouncing around from spot to spot, or watching everything that happened from a safe distance. She knew how to use a look or an episode of recoiling angrily to distance people if they noticed her enjoying camp—that is until she had our daughter as her counselor.

Crystal had watched Joanne's antics over the years. Joanne and Crystal had gradually become childhood friends. Crystal won her over with her gentle spirit. Crystal had just turned eighteen and wanted to be a counselor. We knew she was mature enough for the role. The computer randomly selected Joanne, who was now fourteen, as Crystal's camper.

Joanne once again began her antics and was just as evasive as she had been to other counselors. Crystal came to me almost everyday to discuss and grieve over Joanne.

I reminded her, "You know what these children need. You know what Joanne needs. You are gifted to give it. Even Joanne just needs you to keep loving her, and she will soften. I cannot think of anyone better for Joanne than you." However, as the days went by, I even began to wonder how God would be able to remove the seal around her heart and crack the wall of anger that Joanne had cemented so high.

The day finally came when Joanne realized that Crystal's love for her was not going to be deterred by anything she did. If Crystal was that way, then maybe God loved her that way also. Astonishingly, the thoughts brought Joanne's wall down, and she came to the Lord.

Once she felt the warmth of God's love she started looking at her life differently. She allowed herself to feel hope and joy. Many correspondences over the next couple months were filled with her Biblical inquiries. Questions about why evil happens also started surfacing. Her gift of logic and prudence put things in the right perspective. She was able to soak it all up, her faith growing in leaps and bounds.

We decided to ask her to be a junior counselor the next year. This was the point at which she really started to change. She attended a special junior counselor training camp. There she learned of the bitterness she harbored in her heart toward her mother. It was that inability to forgive that kept her bound and unable to have all the joy God intended for her life.

The training we put each camper through to become a junior counselor takes five months with five meetings with a camp counselor and two intense training weekends. At the training weekend she heard other past campers share how they had decided to forgive their abusers, knowing that this was essential in order for them to be free. She had heard it taught at camp often but could not think of forgiving her mother.

This was a hard step for Joanne. Her memories verified her every right to be bitter. But God's tender prompting finally broke through, and Joanne let go of each thing her mother and father had done. Finally she was free. Joanne was able to flourish in this time of extra study while meeting with a camp counselor. That following summer serving at camp, Joanne grew more in the Lord, learned about a real family, and learned about working together with and loving others.

Joanne had told us, "It was our grandparent's rule since I was little that we had to go to church." Her church attendance began to have meaning now and became even more special as she began teaching the preschoolers at church. She loved working with them and was drawn to work at a daycare center. Joanne found herself there where she could lavish love on children.

Working with them gave her purpose. She also made ties with the adults who were affirming her excellent work. Her hardened heart started to turn to one of deep care for others. As she worked with children, everyone could see her exceptional care, sense of duty, and her attention to the details and desires of the children. Eventually she was asked to be a nanny. Her reputation grew, and she received some noteworthy nanny positions.

One area in which Joanne had to struggle was her tendency to be gruff and curt with adults. Her "matter of fact" approach to blurting out correction ruffled feathers from time to time. She had strong ideals and expected things to be perfect. She also could not accept a compliment well. As Joanne continued to come to camp the love of counselors and other junior counselor's softened her. She listened to instructions on how to curb her expectations of adults. It was hard, and she had to humble herself before God and loved ones often to break free from her gruffness. She grew not only in these areas but in virtue, love, and dedication.

We eventually asked her to be the first camper to join our summer staff in 1997. She began counseling campers. As a counselor she said, "My first camper reminded me of myself." So Joanne did not let her get away with the same tricks but told her, "I used to do what you are doing to me and you can't fool me." In addition to counseling, we assigned her the duties of the assistant nurse. Every child was blessed by her attention to their needs as well as her consistent care. She developed monitoring systems so that she would perform her duties on time and with attention to the details each child needed. She has now served for five years on staff.

Joanne remembers, "I had to raise my support to be on staff and learned to trust God for everything: quitting my old job, venturing out into a new job, and watching God provide through support raising. The new job turned out to be fun and a joy in ministering, watching campers change and grow as I did, year after year."

Some of Joanne's growth was also due to the many trials she endured during the years she was a part of camp. "While I was still a junior counselor my uncle got sick and died of cancer. He had always lived with us. I was a senior in high school when this happened." Her mother was in and out of jail, off and then on drugs again. Taking care of her uncle as he was dying of cancer, depending on her and her grandparents during his final days, took a heavy toll. Several of her endeared nieces and nephews became critically ill and had to be hospitalized several times. Each hospitalization was traumatic. The hardest trial she endured, however, was the revelation that her brother had begun molesting these same children. Her brother had been acting out the same offenses her father had committed against her when she was young.

Amidst these times, Joanne had to learn how to be strong for the rest of the family. She especially wanted to help the children. God was merciful in that she would usually receive each tragic news while she was at camp. Eventually it seemed every time she received a phone call at camp she had to brace herself for another crushing heartache.

Being at camp afforded her to be with those who loved her and who had trained her and seen her through so many other things. Grieving and finding her strength in God became a routine in the many arms of her beloved camp family. It was so difficult for us to watch and to have to feel like we were sending her to face the lions at the end of each camp. But we watched as God used this special time of family problems to make Joanne solid as a rock. She was always ready by the time she went home to courageously help each family member find God's strength. Prayer warriors joined her as she prayed for the strength needed.

Eventually Joanne was able to see that her nieces and nephews came to her own beloved camp for the salvation and the healing they needed. She had to talk her uncles and aunts into letting them go. Each finally came and accepted the Lord.

A major surprise for us occurred when Joanne, who never wanted to leave home, decided God was calling her to go on a mission trip. The strength she gained in the course of time gave her courage to consider going on a mission trip without friends or family nearby. Joanne went to Africa and found her heart broken and filled with love and compassion for the children who not only lived in poverty but without family wealth could not get an education. She made school even more of a priority with the hope that she could return to Africa as a teacher.

Today we are blessed to know that Joanne's strength has allowed her to be the first in her family to attend college. She studied for almost four years at a junior college working full-time to pay for it herself. Then she transferred to California State University at Fullerton where she again worked full time to pay her first year's tuition and expenses. She then learned of the Guardian Scholarship for which she qualified to have every expense completely covered including housing, food, and transportation.

She is currently studying abroad in London and is planning to spend a year in Zimbabwe after that for more schooling. We were surprised again when she decided to attend college in London for a semester as part of the extension program at Cal State, followed by a year in Africa. This same Joanne, who would not venture away from her refuge with grandparents, is now willing to go anywhere for God.

Like many other campers, Joanne became our spiritual daughter. Even our own children considered Joanne their own sister. We could not be more pleased by her growth and healing, by her ability to use her past to help others, and by her strength and perseverence.

I waited patiently for the LORD; he turned to me and heard my cry. (Psalm 40:1)

God has used Joanne to teach me many spiritual lessons. A favorite that I can teach other campers with conviction is that God can get us through anything without our becoming mortally crushed. Instead He can use any horror that has happened to enliven us as useful instruments, who benefit others. I can boldly teach campers that being an ambassador for Jesus by sharing what God has done for them, will turn each thing that has happened into a blessing. God will take what were evils and remake them into a strong conviction, a tender heart, and a testimony. In the end they will say as many other campers have said, "It is worth it." They will be glad they were specially chosen to serve God from their past pain with a powerful witness.

Now if we are children, then we are heirs—heirs of God and co-heirs with Christ, if indeed we share in his sufferings in order that we may also share in his glory. I consider that our present sufferings are not worth comparing with the glory that will be revealed in us. (Romans 8:17–18)

I truly look forward to watching Joanne in heaven as she receives all her rewards for a life that shines for God's glory. She is going to be so surprised by the rewards that God lavishes upon her—rewards that we, who have not suffered as she has, will never taste. But I will be rejoicing and rewarded as I take a front row seat to watch!

Blessed is the man who perseveres under trial, because when he has stood the test, he will receive the crown of life that God has promised to those who love him. (James 1:12)

Chapter Sixteen

In God's Time

In 1982 a thirteen-year-old girl named Angela came to camp with extremely dark, sad eyes. She hid her face with her long, blonde hair. As she began opening up and sharing her life, her counselor could see a controlled, yet overwhelming rage hidden within her. Through the counselors she felt a love she had never before experienced. They did not do things for her just to use her. They truly wanted to get to know her and to help her. She saw their joy and wanted what they had. By the third day of camp, Jesus had touched her life, and a new creation was born. Suddenly her blue eyes sparkled.

During her first camp I asked her how I could pray for her. I shared how God has responded to many campers' prayers as we have prayed over an important issue. I shared how many had received answers to their prayers in just weeks. Her first thought was to be able to go home. She had been in a foster home for five years. We continued to pray for her return home and as each year passed by she would ask us why, though she yearned and prayed to return home, she was unable to.

After returning to camp the next five years, she was able to share of the years she experienced sexual abuse as well as forced involvement in satanic rituals. Year after year, as she continued to return to camp, her countenance became more radiant. We saw the bubbly, enthusiastic personality of this child unveiled before our eyes.

It was after hearing of the satanic abuse that I found myself wondering if God would ever let her go home. The reason Angela finally did share of the satanic abuse was to help another girl reveal the ritual abuse she was suffering. Before this moment I had never witnessed such anguish and horror writhe up in a person, but Angela continued. She knew it was important to bring the other girl out of herself, even at the cost of her own anguish in recalling the horrific memories. She shared in whispers, while her eyes looked around. It was as if she knew someone was overhearing her who would do great evil to her again.

As I realized the extent of the hostilities she had endured, I wondered why she would want to go home to that place of pain and to a father who had nearly destroyed her? For her this place was still her home and that man was her father from whom she desperately wanted love. Later I came to know that since she had forgiven her father, she also was able to want him and her family to know Jesus.

At the age of eighteen, Angela was released from the Social Service System. She returned home just six months after her stepmother had accepted the Lord. God knew that she would not be strong enough to live at home until there was one Christian in the home. It looked like God decided to wait for the right timing before He answered her prayer to go home. We gave her much counsel and prayer.

Angela began to pray for each family member, and God showed her how to reach their hearts. There were three younger brothers and one older sister at home, along with a half-brother and half-sister who were toddlers. She did dishes when it was someone else's turn, cleaned their rooms, and returned anyone's anger with a soft word. One by one she paid for her brothers to go to Camp Alandale (even though campers are not required to give towards camp costs), and one by one they accepted Jesus.

Upheavals in their personal lives kept the brothers from returning more than two times to camp. First one brother than another was sent to their biological mother's home and then returned. Their mother's New Age ideas confused them and hindered their growth.

During this time, Angela met a wonderful Christian man, sought our approval of him after dating awhile and had a beautiful outdoor Christian wedding. As they set up a household, it was not long before one brother after another came knocking on their door after they had been kicked out from their mother or father's home, or a rehabilitation center.

However, Angela and her husband's guidance and enduring love were a constant that eventually led the brothers back to God. They sought the direction of the Lord since the brothers were involved in drugs. Repeatedly, the brothers repented after being thrown out of Angela's home. They received more discipleship but fell away again and again. With each repentance the boys were allowed to return. Angela's patience and mercy were noble and awe-inspiring.

At one point, one of her brothers, Glen, gloriously returned to God and started serving Him on the streets of Hollywood. Having been familiar with the scene he could easily walk the streets and bring runaways and prostitutes into the shelter through which he ministered. The work he did was of great value. He enjoyed the excitement of submitting to the Lord's leading.

Angela's father came to the Lord when Angela's older sister, as an adult, pressed charges against him for the sexual abuse he committed during her childhood. As the court proceedings went forward, her father turned to the Lord and saw God's hand moving. He expected that God would not let him go to prison now that he was a Christian. When he found himself in a cell that he would call home for the next year, he was puzzled and depressed. But a minister came by and gave him a Bible, and he eventually opened it. Soon he was reading it all the time and writing home the things he was learning so that he could pass it on to the family. He soon praised God for giving him a year to fill up on His Word, which was cleansing him and making him strong as a new Christian.

Angela's older sister, who flaunted a rainbow Mohawk hairdo, did not turn to Christ for eight years. During that time Julie gave the family and Angela much anguish and scorn. But she too received the same restorative love of God and has become a new creation. I was able to sit in our front room one day and meet Julie as she and Glen told story after story of God's love and answers to their prayers. Following their testimonies they played the guitar and sang several amazing praise songs that they personally had written. Pure praise and amazement of God flowed from their songs.

At twenty-one-years of age, Angela became our first camper to become a counselor. Her husband has continued to minister to her family at her side, even at camp. They have two children, one named Karen.

Angela's story causes me to realize how God unbelievably is able to redeem and use His children. Satan meant to destroy her forever. Despite the crushing pain that Angela endured as a child, God could take away her despairing spirit. With God, Angela was able to lead her whole family to Christ with prayer and persevering love.

Let us hold unswervingly to the hope we profess, for he who promised is faithful. (Hebrews 10:23)

God saved her at camp. He did not answer her prayer right away. But He gave her an amazing love for her family and the grace to stand beside them. As Angela would call regularly and ask for prayer and advice, I would wonder, "Could I do what Angela is doing?" It was God who put the burning desire in her heart to go home and the grace to stand up under the stress of her dysfunctional family. He is Who made her able.

This verse stands out as I think of Angela.

I the LORD search the heart and examine the mind, to reward a man according to his conduct, according to what his deeds deserve. (Jeremiah 17:10)

The Lord knew He had to prepare Angela in letting her grow a deep yearning for her family. When it was enormous and unselfish, she could be dedicated enough to withstand the long haul that would lead to the salvation of her whole family. He groomed and tested her and, then, when she was ready, He let her have a full, rewarding ministry to her family.

. . . for you are receiving the goal of your faith, the salvation of your souls. (1 Peter 1:9)

Chapter Seventeen

Terrorism: Satan's Tool

We have been greatly affected by the horror that has arisen in our country from school shootings to acts of terrorism. There has been a riveting of our hearts to the victims each time we hear of a new incident. As I watched the eyes of the teens at Columbine High School, and those on the streets around the World Trade Towers, memories of those same looks on campers' faces flashed at me. Our campers have the same kinds of broken, agonizing, questioning looks as they share their stories of abuse around the campfire. The loss of innocence and trust, the knowledge that now there is nowhere to ever feel safe again, and realizing, "I no longer have a home or family I can turn to, how do I cope with this reality?" These feelings are all conveyed in their same desperate looks.

Stories fill my memory. A girl named Darla had been raped repeatedly by an uncle whom, each time, held a gun to her head. He said he would kill her mother and sister if she ever told.

Roy's father periodically beat his family with nail-pierced two-by-fours. He described the backyard where each of his siblings would be forced to watch the others be bloodied by the father's blows.

Another boy, Andy, told of the time when his father beat his sister with a bat after he had tied her up in a laundry bag. He tried to stop his father and was bloodied as he was beaten back with the bat. His sister suffered permanent brain damage from her father's attack, and Andy felt responsible for not being strong enough to help her!

We don't share these kinds of stories very often, but these were the campers who ran through my head. It seems that as the years go by we hear stories of abuse that are filled with ever increasing, unheard of before, violence. Their experiences are traumatic like those teens at Columbine and the victims of the attack on New York City and Washington, D.C.

I am blessed to remember how God turned these three children's lives around and used their pain for good. Darla served many years as a junior counselor at camp sharing her story with campers and telling them of the healing touch of Jesus in her life. She continued to be used by God as He led her into various encounters with young girls her age. As she was moved from foster home to foster home, she shared with everyone how God healed her rage and she was able to lead several of these she met to the Lord. She holds to her faith today at the age of twenty-seven.

Roy, also served as a junior counselor for five years, sharing his story at every camp. Tears of cleansing would run down his face each time as he recalled and shared of his abuse. He was able to reach the other hurting children.

Andy only came to camp a couple times, but I remember the impact camp had on him. His eyes that were dark and glazed over as he shared his story became sparkling and lit up after accepting Jesus into his life. He surrendered his pain to God and forgave his father. He even forgave himself realizing as a little boy there was nothing he could have done to save his sister.

Killing and wars are not something unusual, as our sheltered culture would like to believe. Physical and sexual abuse are common. We all still remember how we felt when the terrorist attacks hit on September 11, 2001. In the same way, our campers remember the smells and sounds from the time of their abuse. We have been impressed with the fact that our campers have so much in common with events of terror. Our nation was at war with an enemy we could not see, one who was hard to locate, one who was very illusive, and one who was able to shatter the lives of so many innocent people.

At camp we are at war with an enemy who is much the same as terrorists. The enemy we fight attacks innocent victims unexpectedly, too. They are assaulted by evil men bent on serving their own passions that master them. These people live secretly among them. The horrors that the campers experience are just as wicked as what we have viewed over and over again on television.

In the children's minds they view the scenes of abuse in the same way perhaps all their lives. The children don't die physically, yet a big part of their hearts (their hope, joy, faith, trust, innocence, and worth) are put to death. As for the future, the lives they come in contact with, those of friends and family, are often affected by the abuse they endured.

Unlike the suicide terrorist, these assailants don't die with them. Sexual abusers live on to kill the hearts of up to an average of ninety other precious children. That statistic is mind boggling but true. Only by a true miracle of salvation in Christ can a child be healed of abuse, and the chain of generational sin be broken. It happens as they are cared for by a God who can thwart the attacks of the enemy, take them through their pain, and erase the effects of terror. This same God is preparing a place for them in heaven for eternity.

His eyes are on the ways of men; he sees their every step. (Job 34:21)

We have an overwhelming responsibility and privilege to be part of the work the Lord desires to do for the abused. We are convinced more than ever that we need to do whatever it takes to reach more of the hurting children of America.

A righteous man may have many troubles, but the LORD delivers him from them all; (Psalm 34:19)

Want to be a part of this venture? Check out how you can get involved at the end of the book in Appendix B.

The Sovereign LORD is my strength; he makes my feet like the feet of a deer, he enables me to go on the heights. (Habakkuk 3:19)

Chapter Eighteen

God's Second Purpose

After twenty years of running Camp Alandale, it became apparent we existed for a second main purpose. This purpose started with a heart-pleading prayer that our board chairman, Hyatt Moore, sent to heaven twenty-five years ago.

At that time, Hyatt's prayer rose out of a heart's desire to reach the many unreached people in the world. Hyatt, being a missionary for Wycliffe Bible Translators, had a desire to go to these unreached people. Yet, he knew he alone could not do it all. As he agonized before the Lord, he was given Matthew 9:37, 38: *The harvest is plentiful but the workers are few. Ask the Lord of the harvest, therefore, to send out workers into his harvest field.*

Hyatt heard God's direction to multiply his efforts through discipling others. The call was clear, and when discussed with his wife Anne, they decided that they would reorganize their priorities and fit in discipleship.

The following Sunday, Robin and I attended a Bible study led by Hyatt. Hyatt promptly invited himself to our home to start a weekly Bible study with Anne and himself. The reason they were open to take on this study was to respond obediently to God's call in discipling others into ministry. This they accomplished lovingly and completely, passing to us the torch of a deep desire to see the Gospel spread. We all thought God would lead us to join Wycliffe to add to those who could be sent out into the "fields." But God's plan was different.

Camp Alandale began five years after Hyatt's prayer. Abused children are not the only ones who have been touched through the years. Amazingly, many counselors and junior counselors have been influenced dramatically in their desire to spread the Gospel. They already have been discipled through participating in the ministry of Camp Alandale, which requires them to learn how to minister through the leading of God's Spirit.

Once counselors have experienced the level of intimacy with God required to effectively minister to abused children, they never want to stop being in some level of service to God. We have heard this expressed time and time again by our volunteers. Over one hundred have gone on to be social workers, teachers, house parents, foster parents, inner city ministry leaders, dynamic church workers, and missionaries to other countries!

Now we see that God's vehicle for answering Hyatt's prayer to see more laborers in the field has been this ministry to abused children. Why abused children? Because ministering to their needs can be as intimidating as going overseas. It requires that our counselors kneel in dependance to God. It teaches them the sufficiency of God's grace as He can be trusted to lead them in any situation.

This was the effect it had on a counselor named Grant Van Cleve back in 1987. Grant had just graduated from college and was challenged by a counselor to volunteer once at Camp Alandale before he began his promising business career. He took the challenge, thinking it would make him a better business man. The counselor encouraged him that the spiritual training he would receive at camp would affect his ethical approach in business.

Through serving a week at camp, Grant became amazed at what it really meant to live daily by the touch of God's spirit. To everyone's surprise, Grant decided he could do nothing less than turn himself over to full-time service for God. It was at this time that God brought his attention to the needy people living in newly opened communist countries. His heart was aflame to help these people. Grant packed his bags, computer, and bicycle. He did not have a mission board or even much of a plan, just the pull on his heart from God to go! It sounded crazy to us. Yet we had felt the same pull on our hearts to go seven years earlier!

When he arrived, he found that many American Christians had responded as he had. The same few cities had a flood of missionaries, so he took his bike and computer on a bus and rode to other nearby towns to list the needs missionaries could address. He then returned to the cities to find missionaries who fit the needs, organized them, and sent them out.

There are too many stories from those years to share here. They show the growth of what is now a large ministry God led Grant to begin. At one point, we received his newsletter that clearly reverberated the nearly forgotten prayer where God told Hyatt to pray for and disciple the "laborers." Grant was asking for the same prayer to be lifted up for him. It occurred to us that God had been answering Hyatt's prayer for over twenty-five years during which time we were oblivious. God had sent Grant to a needy Eastern Europe through a prayer that has affected thousands.

Grant was on the move, ministering in the places of greatest need and tension—the Balkans: Bosnia, Serbia, Kosova, Macedonia, Albania, Greece, Thessalonika, Turkey, Romania, and Bulgaria. While we have heard about the desperate needs in these countries the last fifteen years, Grant was there helping through severe situations. God's light has been shining over many.

Grant has evangelized, raised up his converts, and sent trained Christians all over the Balkans. He held outdoor crusades and concerts; preached in various pulpits; helped the poor, the widows, and the orphans; and started a Bible school to train all the converts. Before some major earthquakes in Turkey, Grant had prepared a team to go help in Turkey because he felt God's leading. Their help came just in time and, consequently they saw revival in Thessalonika (Thessalonica of the New Testament) right before its borders were closed to Westerners.

One of Grant's "students" is reproducing the same results that were modeled by his teacher. Marin has raised up four other men who have adopted Grant's motto to "change the world, together." "Marin's Mighty Men," as Grant calls them have pioneered many new ministries never seen before in Romania. They have separated and are starting their own outreaches, launching more Bible schools, and even reaching out in Turkey (as Romanians they are allowed to enter the country). They started a center in Greece and organized a team that was sent to India. (Americans are only allowed to stay in India three months.)

Grant has been in difficult places for years now: in danger, on the run, or housing three to four refugee families with his own. He comments on all he has seen: "Sometimes in the midst of problems, it is easy to miss the big picture. Before the tragic war with Yugoslavia there were only six Christian churches in Kosova. While in Albania as refugees, many Kosovars met Albanian Christians running the refugee camps and were saved. As a consequence, on their return home, the refugees started forty new Kosovar churches."

This is the real multiplication for which God had first told Hyatt to pray! Hyatt eventually became the National Director of Wycliffe Bible Translators having taken the place of Bernie May and Charles Townsend, the founder of Wycliffe. He has been able to have a profound effect on world evangelism but Camp Alandale was a part of his impact for the world.

It looks like God does not plan to let the multiplication stop. Grant is not the only one in missions building. Kathy Barry, a camp counselor for ten years, is a "camp disciple" who is raising "laborers for the field." She started her own international relief organization and has risked her life bringing supplies and the Gospel to Sudan.

We even have a past camper getting involved in missions. Joanne started coming to camp when she was nine (her story is in Chapter Fifteen). At twenty-one she went on a short-term missions trip to Africa. Now she is planning to go to Bible college and return to Africa as a teacher.

Several camp counselors changed careers and have made significant contributions to the social services system. Over twenty became house parents in group homes. Several more became social workers. Becoming a teacher was an avenue more than fifteen took to impact children's lives. Erica Pedone became a teacher and eventually was hired to plan the curriculum for the state of Colorado's "at risk" students, many of whom are abused children. She made sure that the materials were not out of line with Biblical principles. Shelley (Westmore) Hoss became the vice-president of the Orangewood foundation whose mission it is to help abused children. Several camp counselors heard about the Orangewood Children's Home and became volunteers or were hired to work there.

Camp Alandale is being used for raising up servants for God's work. As counselors work with these children and hear their stories they realize the need of the hurting. For many, the difficulties an individual faces do not compare to the trials of an abused child. As past counselors' hearts become intimately aware of God's call, they see the privilege of their lives being used for God's glory and the saving of many. They develop a passion to give their whole selves for others.

Once they have experienced the suffering of real people, not merely statistics, they cannot be content serving their own needs any longer. Consequentially, after camp many counselors enter professions and ministries working with and for children, or they go back to college to train to enter children's work.

Hyatt's prayer has already impacted at least 50,000 people, perhaps more. There is no way to calculate it, this side of heaven. How could he know the way in which God would work in raising up the laborers for the fields? How completely and extraordinarily does God answer our prayers!!

This encourages me in my own prayers. When I have forgotten a request I have laid before God or when it seems God has been slow to answer one of my prayers, the truth is, He never forgets. He may say no, He may say to wait a while, or He may do more than we ask or expect, but He never forgets! Here is a prayer for "laborers for the fields," that we reminded Hyatt about to his delight twenty-five years later. This prayer came from his heart's cry, led to others obedience, and is growing to cover the world!

Chapter Nineteen

From Fear to Trust

When Don arrived we could tell it was going to be a rough week for this junior high boy. He was cautious and suspicious of others. We could see the pain and fear in his eyes. His counselor, Luke, a Marine, was able to keep his composure with steady resolve despite Don's testing and ability to get into everything. He proved to be quite a handful. As introductions were being made, Don did not want to stay seated. "I didn't come to camp to sit here!" he rebuked sharply.

When it was time for games, Don walked off to get a ball and play by himself. He opened cupboards, tried to go in rooms in which he was not allowed, and was altogether restless. Like a pet who is pacing the floors as he strains his senses to perceive what danger is outside the window, he remained guarded and uptight, not letting people get too close.

The second day of camp, Don decided to go on the hike during "Free Choice Time" (the afternoon time when the campers can choose between three activities—crafts, a hike or Kitchen Kraft). While the hike director was unloading the van at the trail head, Don did not heed the instructions to stay seated but instead, darted out, jumping from one parking bumper to another. These cement parking bumpers were unforgiving so when he missed he fell short with his shin taking the brunt of his fall. The flesh next to his shin bone was gouged three-quarters of an inch deep by five inches long. First aid stopped the bleeding of this frightened boy, but we could see that he was going to need stitches, so we took him to the doctor.

Tending to the care of his wound meant he would miss several hours of the program along with the messages presented. We were wondering why this had happened but rested in the knowledge that God would use it for His glory. Everyone at camp started praying that this accident would "work for the good" as the memory verse that they were learning that day had said: *And we know that in all things God works for the good of those who love Him, who have been called according to His purpose* (Romans 8:28).

Don flat out refused to see the doctor and said, "I don't want stitches, and you can't make me get stitches!" At the doctor's office he was quick-tempered, touchy, and scared. Through all the preliminary checking he maintained a sulky, rock-hard facade. He barked out questions that were contentious like, "Why are you forcing me? You are lying to me. It is going to hurt. I know you won't tell me the truth. Why are you putting that sheet between me and my leg? Why can't I see what you are doing to me?"

We wanted our words to calm him so we gently told him step-by-step what the doctor was doing. We were careful not to let one word come from us that would seem like a lie. We prayed silently and asked for God's patience and guidance. The doctor and nurse decided not to answer him directly but to talk through us. It took both Luke and me to handle him. With gentle, unalarmed responses to all his questions we saw God helping us keep him under control. He appeared as if he could become unmanageable if things went sour.

I assured Don of this doctor's skill and told him I would ask any questions he was afraid to ask of the doctor, no matter how silly they may have seemed. From that moment until the end, every time the doctor left the room Don had something he wanted me to ask the doctor upon his return. I asked every question no matter how trivial.

When the doctor's decision was to do stitches, Don got angry. "I told you I don't want stitches. You can't make me." The doctor turned to him and gently but firmly said, "I have the authority right here on this consent form. You are going to have stitches." When the doctor stepped out of the room, Don let down his guard and wept.

We consoled him and I said, "We won't lie to you, and we'll go through it all with you. We promise to let you know what is going to happen each step of the way."

As the nurse was prepping Don's leg, Luke and I were able to share all kinds of stories of how we saw God take care of us. Luke shared of three times when he had to have stitches. One of the injuries occurred from a failed parachute that dropped Luke to the ground at a high speed.

Luke's story riveted the boy's attention as he said, "I told God, 'Well I guess I'm coming home, Jesus,' then I landed on a house trailer that collapsed under my impact, and it saved my life. I walked away from that with just cuts and bruises." Luke's first-hand experiences allowed him to tell Don each step of the stitching procedure. Then Don knew what to expect, which progressively calmed and comforted him. Much to the amazement of Don, everything Luke said would happen, occurred just as he had said it would. With each of Don's questions, he began looking straight into Luke's eyes instead of avoiding them. It was obvious that Luke was handpicked by God to see Don through this time.

Since Don seemed to be from a gang background, I shared how past campers, who had been part of gangs, had returned home after giving their lives to Jesus to courageously quit their gangs. They felt they could not be a part of the wrongdoings any longer. Trusting God they were willing to go through being "beat down" and other rituals of reprisal for leaving the "brotherhood." I explained that in each case God protected them and none of the threats materialized. "God wants to help you, too!" I added.

When the doctor was done, he said there were fourteen internal stitches and seventeen external stitches. Don sat up, jumped off the bed and said, "What? You are already done? Wow. I didn't even feel it!" I felt the Lord direct me to tell Don that he needed to apologize to the doctor and nurse for being so gruff, as well as to say thank you for the great job they had done. I wondered if this wasn't pushing things a little too far too soon for him. But I felt it was what God put on my heart. So I told him.

You could see he was not used to thanking people and was more accustomed to bullying and yelling at others. "Do I have to?" He fussed. "I don't know what to say," he whispered as he leaned toward me. He walked over to the nurse first and in a street kid kind of way said, "Hey! Sorry. Thanks." I motioned to him again to say more. He went closer, bending to her ear so that others would not hear and said, "You did a great job."

Now it was time to talk to the doctor. Again he stated his thanks simply and even managed to give the doctor a smile! The doctor acknowledged it with surprise, sensing it was heart felt and nodded his head, grinning back with a chuckle.

We were at the doctor's office a total of five hours. It was not wasted or lost time. God used a disobedient act to lead Don to an understanding of His love. God knew it was the only way to reach this boy in time. He was headed down a road of destruction. He had been thrown out of one foster home after another. Violence was brewing in him. This speaks powerfully of the fact that God is in control, able to reach anyone, and even use what is unexpected by us.

In God's economy an incident is used for many purposes. God also let the campers know that He heard their prayers. They had prayed that Don would not have to leave camp early, that it would not hurt, and that he would have a touch from God. When Don returned, he was the center of buzzing attention. He was able to answer their questions of how God had answered each of their prayers. He now felt accepted, part of God's plan, and safe. With animation he told about the fourteen internal stitches and the seventeen external stitches. Everyone responded with "Oohs! and Ahhs!."

The miraculous changes that we saw in Don in that short time were dramatic. That night, Don accepted Jesus as his Savior. By the next day he was a changed boy, free and happy at camp. A couple nights later he shared his testimony of how he was repeatedly abused during his life. We were amazed as he boastfully proclaimed how he was now a child of God! He had suffered abuse from not just one, but several relatives, as well as from caretakers in a foster home. His sharing spoke loudly to the campers of God's ability to reach a severely tough spirit with a hurting soul in one week. He and the other campers spent the rest of the week healing from their pain and learning of Jesus' love for them. They also learned to pray in times of need.

A couple of days later I saw a sweet sight as Don went off on a one-on-one with his pal, Luke. I can still clearly see him briskly keeping strides with the gait of his six-foor-four counselor. He looked up into Luke's eyes with a huge smile, talking and laughing and enjoying the fruit of having a brother in the Lord and together sharing the sonship of God.

Two years later, Don returned to camp. I did not recognize him! He had grown six inches and was fifty pounds heavier. He was now someone I had to look up to in order to look into his eyes. The entire first day I did not recognize him, and he chose not to remind me of who he was. He was great fun to be with, secure, and a part of all the activities. What a difference!

We knew he was a Christian from the answers he gave and from the words he knew to the worship songs that he sang with all his heart. I approached him and remarked, "We sure are enjoying having you here at camp. So, how did you come to know Jesus?" He looked at me in disbelief, "Don't you remember? I asked Jesus into my life here at camp. Look here at this scar. Now, do you remember?"

He lifted his pant leg to reveal the shape of a wound that I well remembered from the first gruesome look I had of it after his fall. It had healed well. Dr. Humenik had done an excellent job of restoration. My eyes welled up with tears, and I hugged our "son in the Lord" who we had lost temporarily when he was moved to a new foster home.

Our counselors usually try to follow up on the campers they have. However, children are moved often in the system for one reason or another. Their new addresses are not allowed to be given to us as a state law prohibits it for the child's safety. Sometimes relatives are trying to kidnap the children or harm them, so the law states that no one can give out their new addresses or even forward the mail of a child in placement. We lose contact with about a third of our campers every year. Luke was never able to follow up on him, yet Don had remained faithful to God, found a good church, and even found his way back to camp.

Therefore, if anyone is in Christ, he is a new creation; the old has gone, the new has come! (2 Corinthians 5:17)

He told stories of being determined to find a good church as we advised him during camp. So when Don got settled in a new home, he found a church where people carried Bibles to service and a place where he could feel the love of Jesus like he felt at Camp Alandale. At his church, he joined the youth group and was part of everything they did. He had his favorite memory verses to share with us and seemed like a child who had gone to church all his life.

> *Praise be to the God . . . the God of all comfort, who comforts us in all our troubles, so that we can comfort those in any trouble with the comfort we ourselves have received from God.* (2 Corinthians 1:3–4)

Looking into Don's eyes, we saw the pain of his past erased. We witnessed the peace and joy flowing from him. This was a testimony of the power of God to restore. Don was a great encouragement to the other campers and staff as he shared his testimony at the campfire. Even if a counselor could not follow up with him, God had been faithful to guide him!

Chapter Twenty

Keri Tells Her Story

Our mom and dad both did drugs. Our dad was abusive to our mom over the simplest things. I remember one time my mom didn't cut his apple the way he liked it, so he started to hit her. I walked downstairs to see what was happening, and he was choking her. In defense of my mom I started screaming for him to stop. He turned from her and looked at me with such rage in his eyes. He grabbed a strap off the wall and said to me, "Do you have something to say?" I said, "No." He said, "Then get up stairs and don't come back down."

My older sister and I went into our rooms and cried as we listened to our mom scream in fear and pain. There were other times when he started to hit her when we were in the room, and he didn't care. I have seen my dad do anything to my mom from slapping her, to choking her, to suffocating her. I always feared that one day I was going to wake up and not have my mom anymore.

My dad wasn't always there. He kind of floated from one person's house to the next. One week my parents were together, and the next my parents were at each other's throats. I thought that it was normal for parents to fight, and dads not to always be there.

There were various times when my mom would take us when our dad was sleeping, and we would go and stay with some friends. We would be gone hours, sometimes days. We even went to a battered women's shelter to escape from our dad. We had to leave everyone and everything behind. We couldn't tell anyone where we were going in fear that our dad might find us. We weren't there for very long. Our mom got us kicked out for doing drugs.

During that time our grandparents got a restraining order against our dad. When we returned home my mom had taken our dad back. We were all scared of him. We thought he was really dangerous, but we loved him with all our hearts.

Our dad came around every now and then. In the midst of my dad leaving us, us leaving him, God had His Hand on our lives. One of the ladies that we would go and stay with would take us to church. We didn't go all the time, nor did our mom attend, but we went every once in awhile.

We moved around a lot and never stayed in one school for too long. There was a time when our mom was so strung out on drugs that she couldn't get up in the morning to take us to school. My older sister and I hardly ever went. When she was already awake from being up all night, she would make us go.

I personally didn't like to go because the kids made fun of me. I did not fit in and was behind in schoolwork. My teachers would even yell at me. There were times when I would throw a fit because I didn't want to go to school. My mom would hit me and scream at me. She would pull me by the hair out of the house. I would show up late at school when I did go and then I would have to tell the school administrator a lie about why I was late. I am sure they knew that I was lying. How often does one have a doctor or dentist appointment in one week, or in one month? I would come in with swollen eyes from crying so much. Every time I would go to school it was a new lie, a new cover up of why I wasn't on time or why I wasn't in school.

When we did go to school our mom would forget to pick us up. We would be there for hours waiting for her to come. One time she never came, and the school called the police to come and get me. The police officer brought me home and found a bunch of people sleeping on our living room floor. He didn't do anything though. Social workers started to come and visit me at school. They would ask me questions about my mom and how things were at home. My mom told us to lie and say everything was fine.

At first I did lie and said that everything was fine, then I got sick of the way things were. I was tired of being made fun of because I wasn't in school. I was tired of not being able to wake my mom up from her sleep. I was tired of there being so many people living with us. I wanted my dad to move back home. I wanted there to be food in the house.

I wanted to be a kid. I didn't want to feed my sisters, change their diapers, give them baths, get them ready for school. I didn't want to take care of my mom when she was sick. I wanted her to take care of me. I didn't want to make my own birthday cake. I wanted my mom to make it. I wanted a mom who was a mom. I was tired of being scared. I was tired of covering for my mom's mistakes. So I told the social worker the truth.

I told her that my mom was hitting us. There were people living with us all the time. I told her that I thought my mom was doing drugs. I told her that I didn't want to live with my mom anymore and that I was scared. I felt hopeless. I wanted to be taken away from my mom. I hated my mom. I blamed her for all the problems that we had. I blamed her for my dad leaving and why I had no friends. I thought it was all her fault. I knew she was doing drugs, and I hated that I knew. I hated that she lied to my sister and me about it. I didn't trust my mom.

When I was about eleven years old, I walked into my living room where my younger sisters were watching television. They were watching an episode of Rin Tin Tin. In this episode they were playing the drums. The beat on the drums was that of doom. At that moment I looked out the window and saw maybe about thirty cops surrounding my house. In fear I ran to my room and could see them with their guns surrounding the house. Before I knew it, there was a policemen standing at the door of my room pointing a gun at me. He started yelling at me and told me to go into the living room.

I watched as policemen tore my home apart. I watched them take my mom to jail and leave us there with somebody who we didn't know and who did drugs. We eventually got to talk to our grandparents, and they came to get us. My older sister and I went to live with our aunt and her girlfriend in Fresno. My little sisters went to live with our grandparents.

My mom didn't stay in jail. They sent her to a rehabilitation place to get her off of drugs. My older sister and I lived at our aunt's house for about six months. Then the two of us moved in with our mom at the rehabilitation place. Our younger sisters stayed living with our grandparents. My mom moved to a different rehabilitation place, and we all moved in with her. We eventually moved out on our own.

My mom was dating a man who she thought she was going to marry. He moved in with us in our new house. Things were going okay, but it was hard for all of us to live together again. We all had so much anger in us towards our mom and each other. Then, my mom's boyfriend went to jail.

After he got arrested everything went down hill. My older sister was getting involved with the wrong crowd at school. She started experimenting with different things in school and with people. I was just trying to fit in and did whatever it took to do so. The younger girls were being ignored. Nobody wanted to deal with them. We all fought not only verbally but physically also.

My mom would still hit us, but it wasn't as bad as before so I didn't think anything of it. We would always say, "You're abusing us," and she would respond by saying, "You don't know what abuse is. Don't you tell me I am abusing you! I'm all you have." So then that would be the end of it.

My mom and older sister would get in really big fights. My mom would hurt my older sister just like my dad hurt her. After my mom's boyfriend got arrested, my mom ran into some of her old drug buddies. She started doing drugs again. People started living with us again. The day finally came when my mom got arrested again.

I called my grandparents, and once again they came and got us. We all moved in with them this time. We had to move everything out of our house and throw a lot away and put a lot into storage. Things were better for us there, as far as a schedule and cleanliness goes. It was hard on all of us because our grandparents were from a different time, and they didn't understand where we were coming from, nor were we used to having structure in our lives. Not to mention the stress that they must have had felt because we were invading their home making it cramped, and putting a financial burden on them. It was just hard.

My mom went to jail for a while this time. While she was there the lady who took us to church when we were younger went to visit her. She led my mom to the Lord. When my mom got out of jail she went to another rehabilitation place. She started going to church and took us with her. All of us went at first. We moved in with our mom, and we were staying with one of her friends. We didn't have bedrooms or anything. It was just a place to stay until she found a place.

One night my mom picked me up from church and we went to the store. I was waiting for my mom to come back. I waited for her for three hours in the car. She never came back. My mom was arrested for shoplifting. It didn't make sense. She stole things that we already had. Not that it makes it any worse, but we didn't need the things that she stole. It wasn't worth it.

So then we all moved back in with our grandparents. All of us that is, except my oldest sister. She went to live with her friend. I lived at my grandparents for about another six months and then moved in with our Christian neighbors across the street that I had developed a relationship with. I lived there for just over a year. All the rest of my sisters moved in with my mom later. I later moved in with my mom, too.

We are all living here with our mom now. Things are still crazy here, but we are only by the grace of God getting through it. It's hard again for all of us to be together. Our mom is clean and really involved with Alcoholics Anonymous (AA) and speaks at prisons and stuff about what she went through. She isn't in fellowship but loves the Lord. Three of us are currently attending church.

Comments by Karen, the author

Keri first came to camp when she was ten, but then because of the upheaval in her life she could not return until she was fourteen. She remembered camp and always wanted to return. When she finally came back, her heart received what it craved as she filled up on God's love. Camp became a time to get her bearings and to unload her heartaches. Over and over she found her counselors at camp helping her to forgive her mom. She always received such deep freedom from Jesus that she could not help but speak of it. At school she was an exuberant witness. Her sparkling personality radiated warmth and joy that no one could miss.

He alone is my rock and my salvation; he is my fortress, I will not be shaken.
(Psalm 62:6)

At sixteen Keri became a junior counselor. From her first camp she was a significant part of helping campers see that God loves them. She shared her testimony at campfire with tears but the reality of the peace God has given Keri was evident. She was able to draw out the most wounded campers. She would share of the current trial she faced and how God was getting her through it. She has always had a high moral standard for herself, so part of her witness at camp and at school included her refusal to do drugs or have sex. She was the strength of her family.

At sixteen she decided to return home even though she was living with a wonderful Christian couple who took her in. We were concerned that the uncontrolled rage that seemed to still exist at home would consume her. She felt the call of God and said He would get her through it. Her concern was for her two younger sisters who would be consumed if no one was there to encourage them in the Lord. So with a mission she entered the "Lion's Den." She accomplished what she set out to do, and at fifteen her two younger sisters regularly attend camp and are just as vibrant witnesses of God's love and grace as Keri.

But it was because the LORD loved you . . . that he brought you out with a mighty hand and redeemed you from the land of slavery . . . (Deuteronomy 7:8)

At camp Keri grew in strength and calling. She wants to someday marry the right man so they can become a Camp Alandale director couple. We look forward to that day. Since she turned eighteen, Keri has been a spokesperson for camp speaking at events and churches. Do you want her to come speak at your event or church? Just let us know. Refer to Appendix B, "How to Contact Us or Get Involved," page 114.

Find rest, O my soul, in God alone; my hope comes from him. (Psalm 62:5)

Chapter Twenty-One

Dana Shares Her Testimony

My name is Dana, and I love the Lord. I am writing this to bring glory to His name for the miracle He's done in my life. My prayer is that through the sharing of my life others will see the difference people can make in a child's life by serving the Lord through this ministry. Not everyone can work directly with the campers. I do not relate to them well, but I know God uses Camp Alandale to change lives. Camp changed my own life, so I volunteer my time in other ways.

May God's tugging on your heart help you consider during this time of reading if the Lord may want to use you for abused children. Serving God through these children means having the *honor* of seeing God change broken hearts into miracles just like Karen and Robin have seen in me.

I didn't grow up with a father, and to this day I do not know who my father is. When I was five years old I was sexually abused by mom's boyfriend. I was scared to death because I had sensed that something bad was going to happen. When he took me by my hand and led me to the bathroom I knew something just was not right. But I was only five, and I knew I could not get away. At that moment I felt utterly helpless and absolutely alone. No one came to rescue me. I was looking at the door and screamed in my head "Mom, Mom, Mom! Where are you? Please help me, please help me! Where are you?"

It was two years before I ever said anything to anybody. I finally told my mom's new boyfriend, and when he took me to tell my mom, she started crying. I said I was sorry. But she yelled at me, I think because she was so upset, and told me to go my room. That night I curled up in my bed and cried and groaned, and I knew in my heart it was my fault. I was a bad girl.

I love my mom very much, and I know she loves me, but at that moment I thought I had done something wrong. For many years I was convinced I was a bad girl, and I became infatuated with sexual desires. Immediately after the abuse I started experimenting with others and became promiscuous. I hated it, but I thought I could never do any better.

Most of my life I used my body to feel the love and acceptance that I craved so much. But I thank the Lord for my mom bringing me up in church and making sure I went every summer and winter to Camp Alandale. In Proverbs 22:6 it says, *Train up a child in the way he should go, and when he is old he will not depart from it.* Praise God for her faithfulness. I recognize that, because I accepted Him into my life when I was seven years old at a Billy Graham Crusade. He's been in my life from almost the beginning of my abuse and kept calling me to Himself as I grew up.

Being in Camp definitely kept me close to Him even though I was running the other way at the same time. Growing up I craved attention, and although I was aware that my neediness pushed people away from me, I couldn't help it. I was always trying to be in the limelight and inevitably became a very loud and obnoxious child. But no matter what I did Karen loved me and never made me feel like I was annoying. Instead she always hugged me, smiled at me, and loved me.

I remember going to camp when I was about fifteen and hating who I was so much that I made up a new name for myself. I told everyone at camp that my real name was Dawn. Karen knew better, but she went along. All week as people would call to me I would rarely respond to the name Dawn. One time as I sat on top of one of the picnic tables, a bunch of kids were calling out to me from another table, "Dawn, Dawn!" I just went on talking at my table. Finally they got my attention when they started all yelling "Dawn, Dawn" together. When I turned around with shock on my face, realizing I had been found out, they all started to roar with laughter. I was mortified.

As I looked up, Karen was lovingly looking at me as if to say, "I understand. It is all right." Soon she was by my side with a warm hug. She did not have to say a word. The love she projected made me feel a lot better. She was always like that. She loved me no matter what I did.

And Robin was like the father I never had. I looked up to him, because he was a man that truly didn't want to use me for anything. He just loved me as a father would. It was unreal!

I looked forward to camp every year because all the people were so nice, and I especially loved the group time we had where we sang songs, swaying back and forth arm in arm, and then watched the fun skits. That was a time where I felt like a family. It was always one of the things I looked forward to the most because people were nice to me, and if I felt that I did not fit in, there were tons of counselors and grown-ups who made me feel loved and made me feel safe. Feeling safe was a *huge* thing for me. They let me be me, and loved me, even as loud and obnoxious as I was. One of the other things I looked forward to was the one-on-one times with my counselors. I got to have their undivided attention! All of us campers would pretend we didn't want to go. Sometimes I made the counselors work to get me to open up, but really I wanted to open up more than anything. I just wanted to see that someone really wanted to know about me. To have someone that showed me love and was nice to me and wanted to spend time with me was unreal.

I will always remember one night with my counselor. We climbed up these mountains at night, and we looked at the stars. It suddenly hit me how *big* God was. It scared me to death. I buried my face in her arms. I cried and said I was scared. She said there was nothing to be afraid of, that God was a big God, but a big God who was full of love for me. She reassured me, and she was so calm. She didn't have any grand words of wisdom or great ideas, and she didn't need to! All I needed were hugs! She made me feel safe and secure and loved. It is an awesome memory of camp that I will always remember.

Through prayer God brought me back to Him. It was a long journey, but we all know God is patient and is never on a timetable. To speak of the person I am today, I will tell you I do not even recognize myself. I have the same body but a totally different spirit. I couldn't live without my regular personal Bible studies, attending church regularly and dependence on the Lord. God has given me such a strong desire to stay pure. My chief desire is to please Him in everything I do. Sometimes when I pray to God I'll just burst out laughing because I cannot believe how much God has changed me. It amazes me a lot.

I have read my diary from when I was eleven years old, and I truly grieve for that little girl. She was so lost, so confused, and her life revolved around trying to find a boy to love her. In between all the garbage that this little girl wrote, there were prayers and praise to God. She recognized that God was always there and He loved her. That recognition came from the people at Camp Alandale and from church where they spoke of God's love for her.

I look at that lonely, lost, needy, confused, sad, little girl, and I wonder how her life could ever amount to anything. And now I can stand before you and tell you that God used Christian men and women in my life to change that sad, helpless, little girl into the woman you see before you today. I praise God for His miracles.

Religion that God our Father accepts as pure and faultless is this: to look after orphans and widows in their distress . . . (James 1:27)

You can bring justice to abused children by visiting them, validating them, and showing them God's love. No great and grand words required, only love. You can minister to them through Camp Alandale. (Refer to Appendix B, "How to Contact us or Get Involved," page 114.) There are not many ministries that you get to *directly* make a difference in an abused child's life. The commitment is small, but the blessing is huge. Prayerfully consider being a part of this ministry and making a difference in a child's life like they made in mine!

Defend the cause of the weak and the fatherless; (Psalm 82:3)

Chapter Twenty-Two

What Happens at Camp?

Each county has a Social Services system set up to care for the "orphans" of our day. Where children once were put into orphanages, today we have foster care. Temporary shelters are utilized for children who are taken from their parents until an appropriate placement is found for them. They may then be put in a foster home where the adult care provider has been screened and trained. These adults, who are usually caring, dedicated individuals, are given finances to provide for the needs of the children. If a child needing placement is determined difficult to handle or if there is no placement available, the child may be put into a group home, where the caregiver may be better equipped or trained. In this situation a child will usually have many more restrictions on his or her freedoms. Group homes are commonly six-bed residential homes or are several "cottages" for six to ten children grouped together into a campus. These are usually staffed by rotating "house parents" who work eight-hour shifts.

So where does Camp Alandale fit into this? The purpose of Camp Alandale is to expose abused and neglected children to the life-changing and healing reality of Jesus Christ and to help equip them to have meaningful, productive lives.

We invite children who are wards of the "State" and are part of the Social Services. We invite children by age groups: 4th–6th graders, junior highers or high schoolers. The Social Services usually tries to find recreational opportunities in safe environments for the children. The children are sometimes difficult to handle, so in a regular camp, a large number of them are sent home for misbehavior. Wounded children need a special type of environment where they feel safe and where a structured program lets them know what they will be doing next. Without it, an instability or fear may surface accompanied with irrational anger and negative actions.

Camp Alandale is structured for their needs and is staffed by trained, loving Christians. We have sent home only four children since we began in 1980. We have attained a very high reputation with social workers since we provide a much needed environment of recreation and training in a safe and wholesome atmosphere.

Also Christian foster homes and group homes who are funded by the State cannot evangelize the children without losing their licenses. They are only allowed to help Christian children grow in the Lord. So when they have a child who is not a Christian, they are happy to be able to send them to Camp Alandale. If the child accepts the Lord at camp, they can take them to church and disciple them after that. Camp Alandale does not take any state funds in order to be able to be free to share the Lord and scriptures openly with children in the Social Service system. We are completely supported by donations.

We also specialize in helping children learn to make appropriate choices, to be productive members of society, and to have a goal of having a healthy family when they grow up.

Many other Southern California counties have heard of our reputation and are asking us to come to their aid. We already turn away as many children as we accept for camp in the counties in which we are working. It is our vision to reach into many more counties since Camp Alandales are needed everywhere.

We cannot reach through our own strength a child whose been hardened by Satan's attacks. Only a special touch of God can do that. But we do provide an atmosphere where the dynamics that lead to changes can occur. When we started this ministry, we had no experience in this field. We had not worked with children. However, God wanted to start something new and different where He reaches His hurting children through human instruments. So, He called ordinary people—inexperienced and untrained—and directed the way to reach the children He was calling to Himself.

Through our involvement in Christian Marriage Encounter as a couple we learned how to become vulnerable and to share the deep things on our hearts. We could see how being transparent changed our marriage. We saw the importance of the same kind of relationship building to reach the hearts of children. So we structured the program to create an opportunity for being open and real with them. Showing the children that we were not like those who abused them helped us gain their trust. However, having an unconditional love from God for the children touches them more than anything.

Our greatest help so we can love the children is having extensive prayer support for all those who participate in the program. Further details regarding prayer was covered in Chapter Fourteen. In Chapter Six, I shared how campfires play a vital role in the workings of God. Here, I want to paint for you, a brush stroke picture of a typical day at camp.

Everyone is awakened by a fun, joyful tune that is played through the campground speaker at 7:00 A.M. Everything in the forest is sparkling and fresh smelling. The kids pop out of their tents into the cool morning air as excitement fills them in expectation of what the day will bring. The campers, junior counselors and counselors have been divided into teams or "families." They sleep in boys or girl tents, cook, participate in games, etc., as a team or family. Everyone is up and ready to eat by 8:00 A.M., and they gather as a family around the outdoor tables. The campers cook their meal and clean up with the supervision and help of the counselors. Family chores are a big part of the program as they are used to model how to be a family member, to develop responsibility, and to find satisfaction and joy in work.

Following this is a worship time in the amphitheater with a comical skit to illustrate the theme of the day. Then the counselors take their two campers for a thirty-minute Bible study on the topic of the day. This is a wonderful time enjoyed in God's picturesque creation as the three look more deeply into His Word.

Soon the game director calls everyone together to play fun and relationship building games. Following this, we meet in the amphitheater again for energized and inspirational singing and a dramatized Bible story that adds to the theme of the day. An important follow-up to the Bible story is the one-on-one time, which proves an all-important time in allowing many breakthroughs to occur. (Refer to Appendix A, page 113, "One-on-One.")

After this we fix another special camper prepared meal, where everyone eats together and cleans up again. Soon the campers are asking, "Is it time for pool yet?" Two gleeful hours in the pool are followed by "Free Choice" time where campers choose between doing a craft, going on a hike, or creating a culinary masterpiece in the kitchen for that evening's dinner. Following this, the campers enjoy an hour-long video or science project with a special guest leader, during which the counselors gather separately to share praises and pray for their campers. The prayer time refreshes the counselors in the Lord so they can end the day in His strength.

Then, once again, it is time to eat. We have meals that a child can make but that have a fancy touch, like barbecue chicken over the open fire and corn on the cob for dinner, or quesadillas with all the toppings for lunch. For breakfast, pancakes with a batch of blueberries thrown in and covered with whipped cream or a fruit syrup made by a camper during Kitchen Kraft time might be the fare. During dinner, everyone finishes learning the memory verse of the day.

After counselors and campers recite the verse, we head off for everyone's favorite time of the day—circling around the campfire! Soon it is dark as we finish singing both spirited fun and worshipful songs. Crazy skits teach more lessons about life and are followed by the most awesome testimonies shared by counselors and campers alike. The testimonies make the whole evening awe inspiring for what God can do in a life.

This special time is made complete by a second one-on-one time where the camper has the opportunity to unload things with their counselor. They are prompted by the sharing of others. Fun games are held around the campfire for those campers who don't leave for one-on-one time.

When everyone returns, we begin a topic that is pertinent to life choices the kids make daily at home. This talk is preluded by a skit which demonstrates the profound and serious elements of the matter at hand. We may talk about abstinence, drugs, pornography, career choices, abortion, etc. After a robust discussion, a soloist closes the night with an inspirational song. Everyone heads up the hill to the tents where snuggled in their sleeping bags, the counselors wrap up the day with a short tent devotion to send their dozing campers to sleep with sweet thoughts of Jesus. They feel safe and loved.

At weekend winter camps, the children are housed indoors, and snowball fights and sledding add to the mixture of fun during the day. Warm times around the fireplace with hot cider make winter camps a completely different experience, especially with the one-to-one ratio of camper-to-counselor. In the summer, we have twenty-four children and twelve counselors. While at winter camp, we have twelve to fifteen campers and just as many counselors.

Whether it is summer or winter camp, each day is packed full of activity with everything we can find that teaches the children about their relationship to God. Whether it is crafts, games, or Bible study, the children are seeing how to live the Christian life through example while they are wrapped in the words of the Lord. Every activity is related to the one before it and to the theme of the day which could be, "From the Pit to the Palace (the story of Joseph)" or "You Have a Mission," or "God's Truth Changes Fear into Faith."

In the past we have said our camp program is just a tool to help the counselors minister. We have known that the impact of the counselors letting God live through them changes lives. And the program is the vehicle. While the spiritually prepared counselor does make all the difference, we now see that the program fundamentally makes a major impact on the campers as well.

A year after our first camp, we found out that a man who had volunteered as a counselor was not even a Christian. We were shocked and asked God, "How can we get the right people as volunteers?"

To our surprise God directed us to a Wycliffe missionary application form. We reduced their ten-page document down to four pages. We wanted the form to reflect out desire to recruit volunteers with the highest standards. We felt God was directing us to find the best counselors to minister to His children who He wanted to love in a special way after what they had gone through. It seemed right but we thought, "Would anyone be willing to fill out this four-page application just to volunteer for a week at camp?"

Our conviction that abused children deserve God's best underlaid the need for the more thorough application. So, certain that it was God who had laid this on our hearts, we printed up the applications but wondered what would happen after we passed them out.

To our amazement, through the years, that application has not only headed off those who we would not have wanted as counselors but it has also brought to us those who are of the highest quality. It seems that in just reading through the application, one realizes that this is a serious ministry. To minimal or non-Christians, it is obvious that they would not qualify, and therefore they never complete the application.

We have always been amazed at the quality of the volunteer counselors God sends. We have been blessed with people with open hearts for God and for the children. We know that their unconditional love and ability to reach the children are from God. They have been called.

Every year we recruit new counselors through Public Service Announcements on Christian radio stations. We also ask our present counselors to invite their friends who they think are strong Christians to be counselors. We make it clear that we are looking for those who have been a Christian for at least two years and are not "Sunday only" Christians but are people who have a growing relationship with God and who have a good working knowledge of the Bible.

We further have them pray for God to clearly direct them to the work. If they feel a call or a desire, we have them fill out an application in which they describe their history, beliefs, and skills. We also ask how they would lead a child to the Lord and in which ministries they have been involved.

After reviewing their applications, and calling their three references, we conduct a two-hour interview where we ask how they became a Christian, and how they would respond to a child in certain circumstances or if they were asked certain questions. The interview is also a type of orientation as to what not to say to an abused child and to use prayer and the Spirit's leading as our main resource. We also ask the tough questions of possible past involvements that would disqualify them, like, "Have you ever abused anyone?" After a week of prayer and consideration we talk and decide together as to whether camp is the place God has for them to serve.

Then each new counselor must be finger printed and cleared by the Department of Justice.

Once approved, they are given an eighty-page counselor training manual to read through two times, and a five-hour audio series. It amazes us how many people actually are willing to go through all of this just because we ask. But we do not apologize for it being a sizeable amount of work anymore. The training they receive is valuable for life as they encounter the hurting and reach out to those in need.

Anyone these days needs to be trained to help the hurting since there are so many who need someone to reach out to them. Therefore, their training is never wasted. In addition, the training materials are interesting and once started easily completed. Once a year we have counselor training where we go over the main areas like discipline, safe touches, program structure, follow-up, etc.

The process is long but produces people who are committed and who are best for the campers. Want to help? Do you want to look at our application? You will find it on our Website. (Refer to Appendix B, page 114.)

All in all, special children who come from horrible situations, come to enjoy a dynamite program where they are ministered to by amazing servants of God. Covered in prayer, the children find great times of wonder through God's love.

Chapter Twenty-Three

nswers to Prayer

It seems appropriate to end this book about God's faithfulness with several short stories that help complete the picture of what I have been painting.

It Snowed That Summer

At one winter camp we had a group of very exciting junior high boys. A few of the campers had been to camp before where they had seen amazing answers to prayer. The weather report had said no snow was possible for that weekend. However, these boys got the other boys excited about praying for the favor of snow from God. It was a wondrous day when overnight six inches of snow fell. The time spent playing in the snow was all the more gleeful. Everyone knew the snow was a special gift from God in answer to the campers' prayers.

The following summer four of those same boys came to camp during the same week in July. Again they desired to see snow fall. They asked if we would let them pray for snow at the next prayer session. We wanted to explain reality, but we thought who are we to say no to prayer. Their faith was not daunted by the fact that this was the summertime, and there was a hot spell going on! We answered them, "Okay, we told you about our daughter who prayed to have her hair go straight, and God answered, so we would not say you can't ask for snow. But you should know that in the twenty years we have had camp it has never snowed during the summer."

That was enough for these boys, and soon they had all the campers praying every time they thought about it. Later in the week a summer shower started, and we had to bring all the campers into the house (summer camp is an outdoor camping experience). When we had everyone sit down for lunch, it started to hail! We had lived in the mountains for fifteen years at this point and knew that hail was a momentary spectacle. When the boys said the hail was our snow, I replied, "Hail only comes down for a couple minutes at the most on our mountain. It is a short-lived phenomena."

However, to my surprise and to everyone's delight, thirty minutes later the hail stopped, and we had two inches of it on the ground! Everything was covered in white! God chose to smile on these children by making the inconceivable a reality. The whole time it was hailing the campers were running around to each other exchanging squeals on how amazing their God was! When the pelting stopped, they all asked, "Can we go out to play in our 'snow'?!"

From Drugs to Ministry

Denise was trapped by her weak impulses. Drugs were an easy crutch since she had seen her mother turn to them to handle her problems. She knew that she wanted what she had found at camp, God's love. However, she succumbed to her old habits shortly after she returned from summer camp to her group home.

When she came to winter camp she heard how to make Jesus her refuge and how to make right choices. This message really helped Denise to realize what she was missing in her life and to desire to live rightly before God. At the end of camp when we were asking for prayer requests, Denise, in a trembling, humble voice pleaded for us to pray that she would stay off drugs and away from the other things that pulled her away from God. She told us that she felt so pure when she was at camp and wanted to stay pure when she was at home.

We put this request in the monthly prayer partner letter that is sent to our prayer volunteers. Denise needed many warriors interceding for her. Since that time, Denise has tested drug free on her bi-monthly checkups.

Margee, a camp counselor and our Vision Promotion Director, decided to start taking Denise to church. On her first Sunday at church, Denise ministered to a woman while they were there. This woman was confiding in Margee about abuse. Denise told the woman how God had helped her through the pain in her own life. Denise's actions made it seem like she was a veteran at ministry.

Margee saw rapid growth in Denise. We all decided it was a good time to ask her to enter the training program to become a junior counselor.

Denise came to the junior counselor training in mid January. She felt honored to have been picked. Denise stood out as one in whom the Spirit was doing another great work that weekend. Her answers to questions and prayers seemed God directed. One week later she helped a friend quit drugs. Her "house parents" (refer to Appendix A, page 112) in her group home began to realize how much she had changed, and she gained their trust. At this same time, she led one of her friends to the Lord and asked Margee if she would take her friend to church, too!

After church one day, Denise told Margee, "It's so strange. The old impulses have faded away. I don't feel a pull or a need for drugs, my old friends, or anything! I am getting pure!"

Denise eventually became the first in her family to ever go to college. She has a good mind and is a business major.

We know that her growth is due to the grace of God on behalf of the prayers of our prayer partners. We would love to have more people praying as a big part of what God does in these campers' lives. If this is something that interests you, please check Appendix B, page 114.

How great is your goodness, which you have stored up for those who fear you, which you bestow in the sight of men on those who take refuge in you. (Psalm 31:19)

Prayers for B. J.

B. J., a camper in junior high, wanted to have people pray for him to find a church. After he went home from camp, he found a church, which changed his life. The once depressed, school dropout returned to school attaining a "B" average. However, he stopped attending that church because he was not as well dressed as everyone else.

He fell back into "sex, drugs, and rock and roll" as he put it. But this time his old lifestyle felt different. It wasn't as satisfying since he knew there was something better. However, in time God not only answered our prayers for B. J. to find a new church but He also provided B. J. with a new circle of influences.

B. J. told me, "I felt like something was behind me, helping me, ever since camp. It was weird. A new friend turned out to be a Christian, and it feels like his family has almost adopted me. I'm there almost everyday. They take me to church all the time. And I'm free. I've stopped everything—smoking, drinking, drugs, sex, and things I don't even want to tell you. I don't have a need for those things anymore."

Both Denise and B. J. said the same thing about the power of God that freed them from their destructive lifestyles. They don't need those secular attractions anymore! God has freed them through the power of prayer!

One of them, when he saw he was healed, came back, praising God in a loud voice. (Luke 17:15)

The Cost of Doing the Right Thing

At one camp, the power of God at work in each camper's life was evident to all of the counselors and staff. One boy who really stood out was Joe. He had been coming to camp for four years. I can still remember his first camp where he fell head over heels "in love" with one of the other campers. Despite his infatuation, he chose to trust the Lord that week. He decided that he wanted to be serious about God. Before he went home the girl he had fallen "in love" with confided in him that she was still being sexually abused. She made him promise not to tell anyone. This piece of knowledge weighed on him at home. He sought the Lord for guidance. He knew the answer, but it was hard to obey.

Joe and this young girl had continued their relationship by phone and letters after camp was over. He knew that she would be upset if he told, and he didn't want to lose her. However, Joe decided that he needed to live righteously and worry about God's approval more than the approval of his girlfriend. When the authorities investigated and found out that his story was true, they moved his girlfriend one hundred miles away for her safety. She wrote and told him that she hated him for what he did, and she never wanted to see him again.

Joe was devastated by the outcome. He knew he had done the right thing for her safety, but it still hurt. He has never forgotten her and wishes he could see her again. Yet Joe doesn't regret getting her out of the abuse. He knows that ever since he decided to please God by obedience, his character has grown as well as his walk with the Lord.

Joe was excited by his growth in the Lord. Tears welled up in his eyes as he told me how much he appreciates what we have done for him at camp. Joe's sincere thanks goes out to all who made it possible for him to come to camp. His pain is healed; his closeness to God is at an all time high. When I asked him if he would like us to consider him to be a junior counselor for next year, his face lit up. He said, "Really! You'll ask me next year? Yes! Yes!"

You may be wondering why this girl was so angry at Joe for helping her out of her abusive situation. Well, many of our campers would rather be at home with their real family than in the system. To them, any family is better than having no family and being moved around from house to house. The abuse is better to them, even if they are hurting, than breaking up their family. They do not realize how devastating long term abuse is and that it will scar them for life. They do not realize their need for a person to speak up on their behalf. If you have hesitated to report a known abuse please contact your local authorities or us for advice. Also refer to Appendix E, "How to Report Abuse" page 126.

It is better to take refuge in the LORD than to trust in man. (Psalm 118:8)

She Never Had a Home

Jamie had been raped by several different men since she was very young. She was placed in the system when she was only seven months old. A bundle of excitement with many talents, this petite, pretty, fragile-hearted girl had lived in over twenty homes. She had been moved frequently due to her great need for attention and her high energy level. She had never felt like she belonged to or was a part of any family until she came to camp. Jamie started coming to camp when she was eight years old. She saw her need for Jesus at her first camp and grew in Him quickly. She was always trying to gain acceptance by offering to help. She wanted to lead singing or do solos. When we would say no thank you to her repeated offers to take over the Game Director's job she would be hurt. We all enjoyed her enthusiasm and loved her, but it was obvious that she had an unnatural need to be in the spotlight.

For two years, she didn't come to camp. We didn't know what had happened to her, but when she finally came back as a junior higher she told us she had decided to check out what the world had to offer. She had put Jesus aside for awhile as she sought acceptance from other arenas. She had gone so far as to get herself on both the boys' wrestling team and the boys' water polo team. These are very physical, contact sports. Jamie had found that she could get the attention she craved from boys rather easily and so she did.

As soon as the bus arrived at camp, with Jamie returning to her "real home" and Jesus, she ran into my arms. Both of us melted into tears.

We were pained to see the wear and tear those two years without the Lord had taken on her. She returned to camp gasping for spiritual air. Slowly during the week, she got her bearings. It was hard work, a spiritual battle, but she had come back to the Lord to stay. As she entered the bus to leave she was waving with a big smile on her face. Suddenly, she crumbled into tears with her arms starting to reach out to me. "I'll come back home, Mom!"

I will betroth you to me forever; I will betroth you in righteousness and justice, in love and compassion. (Hosea 2:19)

A Double Answer to Prayer

Some answers to prayer lift you into explosive happiness. Timmy's answer to prayer is one of those. Two years ago, Timmy came expectant and excited to camp. His heart was ripe for the Lord and yearning for sincere love. A couple of days into camp he told a crushing story of abuse at the campfire. We all reeled with agony for him. In his family abuse was considered normal.

His family moved from hotel to hotel, alley, or underpass to live. He never remembered having much food. Finally he was abandoned on the streets, sexually abused and beaten nearly to death. The agony in his voice over the abandonment was excruciating. He began to sob. But then he concluded his story by saying he had just asked Jesus into his life, and that it felt great!

When it was time for Timmy to go home, he felt unsettled. I had never seen a child so disturbed. I questioned him gently trying to see if current abuse or something horrible at home was the issue. He replied that at last he had a family, all the people at camp, and didn't want to leave.

Timmy had never seen real family love and care. He just couldn't bear to leave it all. We talked, and I counseled him to depend on God. I told him that God's plans for him will always work out for good. I asked him for a prayer request. He said, "I want a Christian 'house parent' at my group home." I encouraged him to pray for himself, too.

He grew in the knowledge and love of Jesus. He began to read his Bible faithfully and to pray for a Christian house parent. We have come to believe that God loves to answer his children's prayers beyond what they ask for. Timmy got two, not one Christian house parent, and they were Camp Alandale Counselors! So Timmy received some of the Camp Alandale family and Christian house parents at the same time!

You will keep in perfect peace him whose mind is steadfast, because he trusts in you. (Isaiah 26:3)

Chapter Twenty-Four

Adult Campers Return

As the years have ticked by since 1980, an unexpected joy has surprised us—the return of past campers with their fiances, families, and memories. I am blessed most by the love of these "camper" parents for their children. I see this as they take their families on tours of the campground and relive their camp years with them, showing them the spots that are most significant to them.

The striking thing is how each of our past campers say almost the exact things! For instance, the most frequent remark is, "You have no idea how much Camp Alandale has meant in my life!" Or, "If it had not been for Camp Alandale, I would have been dead from . . . (the responses vary from suicide, to overdose)". We are shocked that they say such things, but as they give their reasons we nearly fall over in disbelief as we realize that they are not exaggerating. Untold incidences and past situations surface that could have been that person's demise.

We could almost write a script of what they will say after the first hugs and a few tears of joy between us. "You are the only family I ever felt I really had. I felt like I was coming home as I drove up here. Can I go see 'Lookout Rock' or 'Castle Rock' (two special places around camp that are popular hang outs)? This is where I accepted the Lord."

As we walk around camp, next they say, "Oh, wow it still looks the same except it looks so much smaller than I remember!" Then they start touching things as if they were sacred as they say, "I remember this! Oh! Look there is the campfire. I learned so much at those sharing times. Do you still sing . . . (such and such song)?" Then comes the story of their lives and how camp made a difference in what happened to them. Each has been a story you could write a book about.

Jessica was one such camper who returned as an adult. She only came to camp once but could not bring herself to accept God. Her past pain from abuse and her walls closed out all the love of God she felt at camp. But after she got pregnant, became a drug addict, and got involved in all the wrong things, she kept hearing the things she learned at camp in her mind. She would stop short of destroying herself by doing the right thing at the last moment. We praise God to see how He has answered the prayers we have prayed for our campers to be kept for Himself! She finally was exposed again to the salvation message and accepted God. She found a good Bible church and plans to be a counselor someday when she is strong in the Lord.

Another return adult visitor named Tom came to camp two times and then was moved back with his mother. He was never able to come again. He too, couldn't come to a saving knowledge of Jesus when he came to camp. The confusion of a mother who was into mysticism, witchcraft, and such led him to get into all the wrong things. At rock bottom he asked God to come into his life recalling what he had been encouraged to do during his time spent at camp. God turned his life around and led him to minister to runaways, prostitutes, and homosexuals. He was not turned away by the unlovely. He had been one of them and so had a love for them. Our hearts were filled with joy when he shared this with us.

Another named Shawn lives in Texas now with a beautiful Christian wife and three children. His exposure to abuse had been mind-bending and cruel. But just as others had testified, he said camp kept him stable through the horrible things he endured. Yet, he never revealed the things he had experienced at home during the years he was coming to camp. He had accepted the Lord at camp although he only attended three camps and chose God's ways from the beginning. This saved him from so many of the normal pains of wrong choices that the others had to suffer. He led a normal life where he looked for the perfect Christian wife who would love him and his children. When they visited as a family, they so freely cuddled each other and their children. We delighted in God's hand in his life. They became financial partners for camp and have faithfully given every year!

Jennifer also only attended camp twice and never accepted the Lord during that time. About ninety percent of the children who come to camp accept the Lord the first time they come to camp. We thought at first that God was only sending those who were ready. While that is surely a part of it, now we see that abused children already realize they are needy because they have already been broken by abuse. The pride that most have against accepting the Lord is not there. When they have seen nothing but lies and feel their lives are a twisted mess, it is easy for them to acknowledge their need for Jesus. They also are able to spot reality and true love after seeing the counterfeit so often. They can tell when people are telling them the truth and are really sincere. By their second camp most of the rest accept the Lord.

If a child does not receive the Lord the first time they come to camp, they are usually the ones from the severest abusive backgrounds who need to feel God's love a couple times to prove that this is real. Since adult campers have started returning we have learned that if any do not accept the Lord at camp, He is faithful to bring them to Himself later in life. But these have usually made some major mistakes that have brought them to a place where there is nowhere left to turn but to God.

Such was the case with Jennifer. She finally did receive the Lord at the age of twenty-three, and two years later I received a call from her. Her son, Brian, died in a horrible mobile home fire, and she was on the phone calling me within hours of his death. I was glad I was home and available. However, this was the hardest camper phone call I ever had. We both wrenched with pain and flooded ourselves with tears.

Her questions, "Why did God allow this? Did I do something horribly wrong? Why would God take it out on a child?" And comments of, "I just have to have an answer now! We just started going to church, and Brian loved Jesus the most! He was only three years old! He wanted to see the baby that I am pregnant with right now so much, and he'd never get to!" Her expressions of pain tore me apart.

We talked for a couple hours, and then she needed to rest. She called back a few hours later, and we resumed our conversation and prayed. God gave me so many answers for her, and she felt grateful. I explained that God did not hate her. He was not taking it out on her child.

God has a purpose. "God, your Father and Brian's Father is holding Brian right now. Sometimes those who want to see Jesus get to see Him before we will, and now Brian is safe from the pain of this world that bruised you."

I asked her to tell me that she would not turn away from God, but rather go to God with this pain so that it would not embitter her. She had to forgive God and climb into His arms. It was hard, painful work. There was a real battle going on.

Six months later Jennifer, her husband, her five year old son, and her newborn baby visited us. I had not seen her for eight years. We melted into tears in each others arms. She and the family were doing okay and had continued to go to church.

We wish we could write about all of our campers. They are stories of God's faithfulness to the wounded, the power of prayer, the fruit of the countless volunteer hours, and the finances supporters have shared. We are blessed to see the fruit that comes even later in their lives. Someday in heaven we will all share the joys of rejoicing with these campers over all that our God did for them! It gives my heart so much joy!

Afterword

I pray that all who have read this book will find inspiration that does not fade. May the stories come to mind in questioning times and continue to console and encourage. Above all I pray that as a mother cannot leave her child's wound unattended, may God be seen as the loving Father who tenderly cares for all who are hurting. I also pray that everyone will be touched to look around their world to give sustained help to others in pain.

May it be clear that if Jesus lives in a heart long enough, the pained heart can heal. Tormenting memories will fade as the desires of a heart are fulfilled by a sovereign God. Walls of anger will be demolished, and true relationships restored. No one has to live in the darkness of evil if Jesus' light is burning.

As this book ends may we all be encouraged and desire to join the Father in having an impact in occurrences bigger than ourselves. May a commitment to prayer and more Bible study be made. May we all reach out and touch the hurting people around us and may God bless each reader, the counselors and staff administration, and all the children who have been touched by Camp Alandale.

We are grateful to our dedicated major donors who not only made this book possible through their financial support but also gave their time to read and critique the first manuscript. Our supporters are endeared and appreciated for going beyond their regular gifts to fund this work.

Appendix A

Glossary

Counselors These are volunteers twenty-one years of age or older who have been Christians for at least two years. They must have a good knowledge of the Bible and a strong walk with the Lord.

Emancipated Being released from State control in the Social Services System at eighteen years of age to care for oneself.

Foster Home A volunteer family who is licensed and paid to care for children without a home or family due to abuse, the jailing of parents, etc.

Free Choice The afternoon time when the campers can chose between three activities–crafts, a hike, or Kitchen Kraft.

Group Home A house in a neighborhood or an institutional style campus where difficult to handle children are placed for care. Trained staff usually rotate on eight hour shifts.

House Parents The staff of group homes are sometimes called "house parents." The idea is for the children to feel like they have a family. House parents used to be couples but now are mostly single people. Many group homes have switched over to just calling their paid employees who care for the children "staff." Because of heavy turnover rates, it has been decided by some that the staff should not have a bonding relationship with the children.

Glossary

Junior Counselor A junior counselor is a young adult, sixteen to twenty years old, who comes as a volunteer to minister to the children by being fun at camp and by helping with behind-the-scenes work. These are usually past campers or the most solid Christian teens from area churches.

Orangewood A temporary shelter in Orange County, California, for children who have been taken from their homes or off the streets or who have been terminated from a placement for various reasons.

Placement Referring to being placed somewhere in the system as a foster home, group home, health facility, a relative, etc.

One-on-one Every day counselors take each of their campers for a half-hour to talk. It is a time to discuss the topic of the day, let children get things off their chests, to pray, or do whatever the Lord leads.

Social Services The State system that cares for displaced children by providing care in foster or group homes.

The System Short term for the Social Services System.

Appendix B

How to Contact Us or Get Involved

Camp Alandale
P.O. Box 35
Idyllwild, CA 92549-0035
(909) 659-5253
Fax (909) 659-2353
Karen's E-mail: Karen@CampAlandale.org
Camp's E-mail: CampAlandale@CampAlandale.org
Website: www.CampAlandale.org

Receive information from our Website.

E-mail, call, or write us. Give us your name address, telephone number, etc., along with your request or questions.

If you are interested in how you can become involved at camp, this appendix includes many, but not all, of those different ways.

Becoming a Counselor

If you want to be a counselor, an application can be downloaded from our Website, or call us and we will mail one to you. At the present we are only looking for volunteers who live in the Southern California area. Eventually we want to go nationwide, but for now we are recruiting those whose residence is in this area to facilitate follow-up contact with those campers that we desire our counselors to stay in touch with. Our counselors are required to be Christians for at least two years, committed in a daily walk with the Lord, have good Bible knowledge, and feel a call on their lives to minister to abused children. Past experience working with abused children is not required, but we require fingerprinting of all counselors. We provide training materials and sessions.

Becoming a Junior Counselor

Junior counselors are young people between the ages of sixteen and twenty years old. In order to apply, they must be sixteen by January prior to the summer they wish to serve. We look for those who are the strongest Christians in their youth group and who have shown an ability to minister. All applicants must: (1) complete a junior counselor application. All requests for applications must be received by November of the year prior to summer camp. (2) have their youth pastor complete a recommendation form, (3) commit to volunteer to serve for at least two camps in the summer, (4) attend at least one (though we prefer two) of the two training sessions that are scheduled in January and May, and (5) complete five Bible studies that will qualify the applicant to be a junior counselor.

Mailing List

You can request to be placed on our mailing list via E-mail, a telephone call, or writing to us at the addresses on the previous page. Those who are on our mailing list receive four newsletters and four board chairman letters each year.

Prayer List

You also may request to be a prayer partner and receive a bimonthly prayer letter that will share of camp and camper prayer needs.

Donations

Send all donations to the P. O. Box address on the previous page. Your donation will be receipted, and you can claim a deduction as we are a non-profit corporation. Information about audits, annual reports, etc., can be sent to you upon request.

Becoming a Camp Director Couple

We are looking for married couples who have young children or are planning to have children and are strong leaders who are able to teach the Word of God to youth as well as adults. Those with a long, consistent Christian walk are chosen to begin in training as assistant camp directors with the plan that, with our assistance, they will eventually begin a Camp Alandale in another county. We have couples serve as volunteer counselors at several camps first so that we and the couples can see if camp is truly their calling. We are looking for long term relationships. We only have couples as camp directors because abused children have a deep need to see marriage and family life modeled to them. Write or call for more information.

Becoming a Part in Other Ways

If you cannot be a counselor but wish to help in a tangible, hands-on way, there are other ways to be involved. You may consider joining one of the several "Women 4 Orphans" groups whose main emphasis is organizing and hosting events to increase awareness of child abuse and Camp Alandale's ministry to these victims. Or you may want to help our Vision Promotion Team as they reach the Christian community in offering opportunities for serving the children who have suffered from abuse or neglect. Perhaps you would like to use your professional skills (i.e. of a building contractor or a lawyer) to aide the ministry. All sorts of talents and gifts are needed. Feel free to let us know how you would like to help or contribute.

Keynote Speaking, Retreat Speaking or Concert Booking for Your Church or Other Organization

We want to let you know that Karen has been trained to present practical and inspirational messages for retreats whereby she intertwines encouraging camper stories with Scriptures and themes such as: "How to Handle Trials" or "Forgiving." These presentations can be of any length for a luncheon to a full-day seminar. Karen also has a beautiful singing voice with which God has drawn campers to Himself for years. In a presentation, she shares a camper story and accentuates it by singing a song.

In addition, the camp staff are available if you desire to have a speaker at a meeting. Our presentations are given without an "ask" of finances, but materials will be offered and books will be for sale. Love offerings are another option.

Robin and Karen (Founders and Executive Directors) and other Camp Directors are available to share camper stories that are inspiring and motivating for people who attend church services, Bible studies, college and career groups, senior high youth groups, Christian and secular, etc. You can request a brochure or CD of sample speaking and concert performances for review.

May God lead you as you look into becoming a part of this ministry.

How to Send a Child You Know that Needs Camp

We accept children to camp who have a social worker in Orange or San Diego counties. In the future we plan to expand to all Southern California counties. Just call with the child's name, address and phone number, and the name of their social worker so we can add them to our invitation list. These new children are invited to the next available summer camp. We do not start children at winter camps since a weekend is too short a time to do the work that needs to happen at a first camp.

Appendix C

Statistics of Abuse and How Camp Helps

National Statistics (Source: 1999 National Child Abuse and Neglect Reporting System—Feb. 2002)

- Everyday three children in the U.S. are murdered by a parent or caretaker.
- 18,000 children are permanently disabled every year.
- 565,000 are seriously injured every year.
- Nationwide three million children were reported as victims of child abuse and neglect in 1999.
- As of September 30, 1999, there were 568,000 children in foster care.
- There were an estimated 826,000 victims of maltreatment nationwide.
- The 1999 rate of victimization, 11.8 per 1,000 children.
- Almost three-fifths of all victims (58.4%) suffered neglect, while one-fifth (21.3%) suffered physical abuse; 11.3% were sexually abused. More than one-third (35.9%) of all victims were reported to be victims of other or additional types of maltreatment.
- Three-fifths (61.8%) of perpetrators were female.
- Almost nine-tenths (87.3%) of all victims were maltreated by at least one parent. The most common pattern of maltreatment was a child victimized by a female parent acting alone (44.7%).
- In cases of sexual abuse, more than half of victims (56%) were abused by male parents, male relatives, or other males.
- An estimated 1,100 children died of abuse and neglect, a rate of approximately 1.62 deaths per 100,000 children in the general population.
- One in four female children will be molested by age eighteen. One in six males will be molested by age eighteen.
- The Urban Institute reports that in fiscal year 1998, the total spending (federal, state, and local) for out-of-home care was estimated to be at least $9.4 billion (Bess, Leos-Urbel & Geen, 2001).

Orange County Statistics (Source: Child Abuse Registry Statistics for 2001)

- In 2001 nearly 25,000 cases of abuse were reported in Orange County.
- 18% of cases reported were for sexual abuse.
- 32% of the cases were for physical abuse.
- There are over 4,000 children living in foster homes and group homes in the county.

Camp Alandale Statistics (as of December 31, 2001)

- 22 Years of Ministry (1980–2002)
- Over 2,500 individual children have been to camp.
- Most attend camp for two or three years, some as many as ten years.
- Most of those who are not Christians receive Jesus the first time at camp.
- Over forty campers have become junior counselors.
- Twelve campers have become counselors.
- One camper has been on summer staff for four years.
- One camper joined the permanent staff in 2001.

Volunteers

- Four hundred and fifty counselors
- Three hundred junior counselors
- Two thousand prayer partners, helpers, and supporters
- Sixty "Women 4 Orphans" members

The Vision

The purpose of Camp Alandale is to expose abused and neglected children to the life-changing and healing reality of Jesus Christ and to help equip them to have meaningful, productive lives. There is a crisis in our country of abused children reeling in pain, striking out at others or themselves. God is the only one who can completely heal their debilitating wounds. As we see this great need in our country as outlined in the statistics, we know we have a solution to this crisis. Therefore we have set a goal of raising up five Camp Alandales in five different Southern California counties by the year 2010. The camp directors of these camps then will have the responsibility to raise up new Camp Alandales from qualified couples that they train in their camps. When we reach this point, the number of camps can grow exponentially across the nation.

"The vision" is not ours. We are only stewards of the vision and the ones who get to participate in it. The vision belongs to the Lord! We also believe that we can do nothing without prayer and obedience. Everything should be covered with prayer and in step with the Bible and the Lord's leading.

We know God is telling us to look for new camp director couples to train and send out. Every few years the vision will require new buildings to be constructed. The financial need will mushroom as we reach more and more children. To do all this we need more people to spread the word so God can touch other hearts to become involved. Would you like to help?

Each person has been given a purpose in life by God, something that they are to do. We want to find those who God has chosen to be a part of Camp Alandale. Our method of finding who God would have to be a part of the vision and the ministry of giving or volunteering is to take our unique purpose and find those whose purpose matches ours. Each person's purpose is like a "tuning fork" within them.

We need to ring our own tuning fork and see if it resonates with other people's. We can find others whose hearts are on the same frequency, and these are the ones who should be a part of our ministry. Some people have never taken the time to find out their purpose in life, so we have the joy of helping them see if camp is a purpose for which God would use them. We pray God will use this book to help people find if they are to participate in Camp Alandale. Is our tuning fork resonating with you? Contact us. Refer to Appendix B.

He who is kind to the poor lends to the LORD, and he will reward him for what he has done. (Proverbs 19:17)

A generous man will prosper; he who refreshes others will himself be refreshed. (Proverbs 11:25)

Appendix D

How to Help a Hurting Person Without Getting Hurt

Often people tell my husband Robin and me, that they are amazed by the many years we have been able to minister to the abused as Executive Directors of Camp Alandale. By reading these stories some of you may desire to help those hurting people who God sends your way. For those of you who do, I want to give you some practical guidelines to help you avoid a parasitic or overwhelming relationship.

A person who needs professional help can put you in an overwhelming relationship. Parasitic relationships are created when you try to help someone and succeed in helping him only to have him become dependent upon you. This individual drains you of all your resources as you try to live for both yourself and the other person. Parasitic relationships are harmful to both parties. The one helping may exhaust himself and his resources by constantly giving. The helper then may pull back ending the relationship poorly, never desiring to help another again. The individual never learns to grow and mature on his own and continues to blame others for his problems in life. I wish to share a story and then some hints about reaching out.

James and the Giant Dilemma

Over the years there have been some intense times with campers. A few of them have come face-to-face to us and challenged our authority. In these situations, the Lord has given us firm, but loving words to handle the situation. Gratefulness floods our hearts. However, the hardest confrontations are with those campers who are not mentally coherent.

Such a boy came to a high school camp. When his counselor told us that James was not eating, and he needed someone to get things under control, we did not know the extent of this boy's problems. At counselor prayer time it was decided that we should take a soft approach and let me, the mother figure, talk to him.

When dinner came, James left the table declaring that he was not hungry. I saw him and decided it was the time to talk to him. Even though I was unsure of how to act or what to say, I remembered that in my weakness God is strong. Also, the thought of the many people praying for this camp gave me the strength to face James. I knew that I was not facing him alone.

As I approached James, a warm feeling for him grew in my heart. I smiled and softly said, "Well, what are you doing over here all alone?" He acted like he was in trouble, and I just tried to disarm him. "I really hope you are having fun at camp. This is your place to get away and be happy."

He really responded to that statement, and all his beliefs and anxieties poured out! He explained first that life was the pits, and he did not expect to bother living beyond the age of eighteen. In his morbid state of mind, he declared that he loved this mountain area because there were so many high places that a person could jump from to take his life.

I asked James why he thought life was so awful. He explained that he had messed up his mind and body sniffing glues and doing other drugs. Now he was on fifteen medications daily just to keep him from hurting himself or others. James didn't want to live like that, and so he didn't want to live.

I was amazed by the calmness I felt and exuded to him as he talked. It didn't even bother me when he mentioned he had tried to slash several people with knifes, his favorite weapon. Even though this was a tough child, I was amazed that I did not feel in this case like turning and looking for reinforcements. My mind and heart were intent on reaching him. God was being sufficient in my weakness. Nevertheless, I wondered if we would be able to responsibly keep him for a whole week at camp, considering the safety of others as a whole.

James began to talk about not liking to eat since his medications made food taste bad. He had lost sixty pounds in the last year. I told him all this saddened me. I went on to say that I knew God had an answer for how he could handle living like this, and I wished he would look for that answer at camp. After all, that was what camp was for.

James was taken back by my comments. He looked at me as if to say you don't think I'm a hopeless case? I said I really wanted him to try eating something that night. Half a piece of chicken was all I could get him to agree to after reviewing the menu. He caught his thoughts again and said he did not know if he could eat anything the next day. But I said, "Just eat this one meal, and we will talk in the morning." The next day I was at each of his meals, and he agreed to eat a certain larger amount than the time before.

For the rest of the camp I intentionally sought to not prod him but congratulated him on how much he ate. He ate on his own. But I was always there speaking kind words in his ear. As we hiked or did other activities, I would repeat the fact that God was real and He could still make something of James' life.

The look in his eyes was so amazing. I could see he wanted to believe what I said and he searched my eyes deeply each time I would talk of hope. He wanted to hear it. Each day James would become more normal acting. His preoccupation with death, suicide, and life being hopeless greatly subsided.

Another blessing to James from God was the way his counselor and all the others could now pour themselves into this boy. His counselor did not have a clue of how to handle the situation. It was his first time at camp as a counselor! He was so willing to let God use him for this boy that he just prayed continuously. As his counselor saw God act in response to prayers, he grew mightily in the Lord, with deep thanksgiving, for the experience.

What I brought away from the experience was a deeper belief that God is able to act powerfully even when we are afraid we can't handle the situation. I truly believe God can use any of us to accomplish His will in the lives of the "unreachables," if we just trust him by walking wherever He leads. I am constantly receiving a new confidence in God's sufficiency, especially when I know there are many praying for campers and our work with them.

Guidelines to Avoid Parasitic Relationships

The above story is an extreme case, but you may be called to help someone in such an impossible situation. Remember that you need to trust in God's sufficiency and use the resources of His Word, wise counsel, and His Holy Spirit. A team of prayer warriors is vital to being able to be used as an instrument of God.

Be aware that many times, God has us just do a small part in someone's life during a short period of time. For example, we never saw James again. But I know God had something that He wanted this boy to know, and camp was the place for him to learn it. Sometimes we never see the result of our actions. We can trust in God's sovereignty as He knows what He is doing for His children.

Some of you have a call on your life and are able to reach people when others are unable. This may be because you are a wise and practical person who does not let people take advantage of you. You may be the person who God calls to help for a longer time period. Or you may have a big heart, and often this leads people into parasitic relationships where you can become "burnt out."

This can be avoided. You need someone who will be a sounding board to whom you *listen*. For example, I would answer the phone twenty-four hours a day for a person in need if it were not for my husband who is my coach. I need to have someone who is able to tell me when I am "helping too much." I have to check if I am enabling someone to depend on me instead of enabling him to grow on his own. If the people I am trying to help stop putting in effort and they would crumble if I was not there, then things are not in balance. Neither are they progressing.

There are questions to ask when you are called to help another. Am I helping or being his idol? Am I trying to control him? Have I prayed about this enough? Am I remembering this is not about me, but about serving God? Am I serving God or men? Am I seeking to be humble as I serve another? Do I have unreal expectations? Am I imposing my own dreams and desires on this person? Do I know what he needs? Have I asked and really listened to a coach? Have guidelines been made and held to? Have goals been discussed and plans made for how and when to reach him or her?

This list is not exhaustive since there are so many circumstances that can arise. The point is that you need to ask yourself hard questions before and while reaching out to another. Not only do you need to ask yourself, but you also need to have someone keep you accountable. You need the objective viewpoint of another to help guide you. Review your written guidelines and goals. Have targeted dates for completion. This will help you successfully serve the needy.

When I start to help someone on a long-term basis, I know it is okay to hold her hand for a short time in order to get her started out of the mire. But I also know that a high level of help must gradually decrease and eventually become minimal in order to maintain a healthy relationship.

The responsibility for her life must be transferred to that person. We have all heard the analogy of teaching how to use a fishing pole, instead of giving a person a plate of cooked fish all the time. At first I may need to show her how to bait the hook, how to hold the rod, how to cook the fish, but this should only be done once or twice. Then I need to let the person do what she has learned from then on.

Guard yourself from feeling guilty if the individual doesn't want to change. If he is unwilling to take the responsibility to learn how to live his life, then your responsibility to help stops. If he makes consistently bad choices after your care and guidance, your responsibility to help stops. Up front rules need to be established, and time limits laid out that are not optional. If you say, "I will let you live in my home and help you get a job if you get sober." Then if the person does not get sober, he is out on the street by his own choice.

I always try to show people how their choices determine whether or not they have my help. They take my choice away to want to help when they choose to do things in which I will not support them. For instance, living with a girlfriend, not looking for a job or being able to keep it, joining a gang, or doing drugs are all taboo. Going back to the analogy, if they do not choose to fish, my responsibility ends.

Two Scriptures need to be kept in balance:

> *Do not withhold good from those who deserve it, when it is in your power to act.* (Proverbs 3:27)

> *For even when we were with you, we gave you this rule: "If a man will not work, he shall not eat." We hear that some among you are idle. They are not busy; they are busybodies. Such people we command and urge in the Lord Jesus Christ to settle down and earn the bread they eat. And as for you, brothers, never tire of doing what is right. If anyone does not obey our instruction in this letter, take special note of him. Do not associate with him, in order that he may feel ashamed. Yet do not regard him as an enemy, but warn him as a brother.* (2 Thessalonians 3:10–15)

You also need to be cautious of your own weaknesses. If your whole life starts to revolve around the person you are helping, you will get drained. You will feel used and may burn out. This is not healthy for the one you are helping or for yourself. It will strain the relationship.

It has been my own experience in parasitical relationships, as well as to many I have talked, that in trying to do the Christian and right thing, many drown. They end the relationship poorly and never want to help a needy person again. However it is often our own fault for letting someone become a parasite.

If you are not equipped to handle someone, that's OK. The police and mental health authorities may need to get involved. They are the custodians of maintaining order. It is their duty to help. Don't think that you have to do it all on your own. It is irresponsible to think that your "charm" and established relationship will be able to control an unruly person, even if he is a child. If a situation seems volatile, never assume that you can stop the eruption of rage. For instance, if a weapon is shown or used to threaten, it is absolutely the time to call the authorities. This person has crossed the line criminally. Being heroic at this point is only good movie drama, not reality.

All of this is important to consider. I know what I have been called to do, and I have a team with whom I can work. I can go in confidence, as I mentioned before, because of the many who are praying for the ministry. So remember the body of Christ for your own ministry. Know where you are called. If He is calling you, then boldly go in His strength. He will provide the way and the strength.

Consider that God may want you to join or assemble a team for a task. He usually is not looking for a bunch of "Mavericks," but He effectively can use the Body of Christ as a team. Have many pray for you. Seek advise and seek God's wisdom and patience. Know that God can do all things even through you. At the end there is the joy of participating in work that is bigger than ourselves.

Religion that God our Father accepts as pure and faultless is this: to look after orphans and widows in their distress and to keep oneself from being polluted by the world. (James 1:27)

Who is wise and understanding among you? Let him show it by his good life, by deeds done in the humility that comes from wisdom. (James 3:13)

Remember this: Whoever turns a sinner from the error of his way will save him from death and cover over a multitude of sins. (James 5:20)

If anyone speaks, he should do it as one speaking the very words of God. If anyone serves, he should do it with the strength God provides, so that in all things God may be praised through Jesus Christ. To him be the glory and the power for ever and ever. Amen. (1 Peter 4:11)

Appendix E

How to Report Abuse

If abuse is going on right now, it is an emergency. Call 911.

To report suspected abuse or neglect, call the Child Protective Services number appropriate to the county in which the child resides:

Los Angeles County	(800) 540-4000
Orange County	(714) 938-0505
Riverside County	(800) 442-4918
San Bernardino County	(800) 827-8724
San Diego County	(858) 560-2191

Crisis Intervention Hotlines

CHILDHELP USA National Child Abuse Hotline   (800) 422-4453
1-800-4-A-CHILD, a national hotline dedicated to the prevention of child abuse. The hotline is staffed 24 hours daily with professional crisis counselors who utilize a database of more that 65,000 different emergency, social service and support resources nationwide.

COVENANT HOUSE   (800) 999-9999
www.Covenanthouse.org
Offers short and long term assistance to young people who are abandoned, victims of child abuse, drug abuse, prostitution, etc. The Ninepin, a 24-hour-toll-free hotline, handled more that 84,100 crisis calls last year from troubled youngsters and parents.

NATIONAL RUN-AWAY SWITCHBOARD   (800) 621-4000
Web: www.nrscrisisline.org
E-Mail: info@nrscrisisline.org
A 24-hour hotline for youth eighteen years and under, as well as their families, providing crisis intervention, information and referral service, mes-

sage and conferencing services between youth, their parents/guardian, and/
or an appropriate agency.

YOUTH CRISIS HOTLINE (800) 448-4663

1-800-HIT-HOME, a national 24-hour Christian referral service providing crisis intervention for runaways and parents of runaways, rape and
abuse victims, drug and alcohol addictions, etc. We provide Christian assistance to find shelters, teen-centers and transportation to callers under
the age of eighteen. This is a volunteer program. If you are interested in
helping, call (858) 292-5683.

CHILD MOLESTER IDENTIFICATION HOTLINE (900) 463-0400

Parents concerned about a person's behavior around their children can
call the California Department of Justice to obtain information about regis-
tered sex offenders. ($10 Service Fee)

If you are interested in additional copies of this book

Send a $12 donation to:

Camp Alandale
P.O. Box 35
Idyllwild, CA 92549-0035

Include your name, address, and telephone number.
Make your check payable to Camp Alandale.

For five or more copies, we suggest a $9 donation for each.

Call us about suggested donations for other quantities,
or for books to be used for promotional purposes.

(909) 659-5253

We will absorb the shipping and handling charges.